THE GREAT AWAKENING

Temple Teachings from the

Higher Realms

Volume XII

Sister Thedra

Copyright © 2021 by Halls of Light, LLC

All rights reserved. This book or any portion thereof may not be reproduced or used in any manner whatsoever without the express written permission of the publisher except for the use of brief quotations in a book review.

ISBN: 978-1-7366487-1-1

By Mine hand I have Blest this Book,
I dedicate it to All who seek the Light.

To the Reader

This book is only a portion of the teachings and prophecies that have been given by Sananda, Sanat Kumara, and others of the higher realms, and Recorded by Sister Thedra.

Contents

LIFT UP THINE EYES 1

THE EMERALD CROSS 13

BORN - THE VIRGIN SPIRIT 28

BORN 38

STEPHANI 69

"PRAISE HIM..." SORI SORI 83

EASTER SUNDAY 123

ONES ARE IN OUR MIDST 195

SORI SORI 230

Mission Statement 235

Sananda's Appearance 236

Authority to Use the Name Sananda 237

About the Late Sister Thedra 239

Esu Jesus Sananda

This reproduction is from an actual photograph taken on June 1st, 1961, in Chichen Itza, Yucatan, by one of thirty archaeologists working in the area at the time. Sananda appeared in visible, tangible body and permitted His photograph to be taken.

LIFT UP THINE EYES

Sanat Kumara speaking unto thee--

Beloved of my being- I come unto thee this day that ye may be given that which has been kept for thee- and it is for the good of all mankind that I come---

Now Ye shall say unto them in my name that they shall be as ones which have the law given unto them which is given unto US-- I say WE which have gone before thee to prepare the way before thee have followed these laws- or the <u>ONE LAW</u> to the letter--we break it not-for we have the WISDOM of the INITIATE---

I say ye have been given the key to the KINGDOM of GOD- if ye will but see it--

I say-- WILL YE NOT WALK IN THE PATH SET BEFORE THEE? And ye shall be glad forevermore---

Rejoice that it is now come when these things shall be revealed unto thee- and ye shall be glad throughout all eternity that ye have been delivered out---

Now it is come when great stress shall come upon all the peoples of the land--and they shall fall under the yoke of oppression-- and I say unto thee- MY PEOPLE - LIFT UP THINE EYES UNTO THE HILLS-LIFT UP THY HEART UNTO THE EVERLASTING SHRINE - WHICH IS THY OWN LIGHT WITHIN THE INNER TEMPLE WHEREIN YE SHALL GO--WHEREIN ALL THINGS SHALL BE REVEALED UNTO THEE---

I say this is the ROYAL ROAD upon which ye have come-- I say ye are now entering into the portals of learning- and ye know not what lies ahead of thee- and ye see not beyond the veil---

Ye go in and out from thy place of abode with no vision of that which is to come - ye are blinded by the veil of Maya-- Yet- MY PEOPLE! LIFT UP THINE EYES AND OPEN UP THY HEART AND YE SHALL BE TOUCHED AND QUICKENED AND YE SHALL COMPREHEND THE LAW- AND YE SHALL WALK WITH SURETY- AND WITH DIGNITY---

And ye shall not make a mockery of that which has been given unto thee for thy own welfare---

I say ye shall not mock me--ye shall not make a mockery of the law set down before thee- ye shall not give unto me the BITTER CUP-Ye shall not persecute my prophets-- ye shall bless them- and give unto them as they would give unto thee- ye shall give unto them food and drink for they are sent unto thee even as I am sent-for as I receive of GOD the Father so do I give unto them and they in turn give unto thee.

I am now come that there might be great light among thee O MY PEOPLE- be ye alert and hear me! For I am come that ye may be delivered out before the great day of sorrow---

I come that ye might be up and about thy preparation that ye might be brought out of bondage---

HEAR ME- HEAR ME! ALL YE PEOPLE OF THE EARTH!

I stand ready to give unto thee as ye are prepared to receive- and I say - ye have received little - yet my store is boundless- and ye comprehend not the fullness of the Fathers house---

ARISE and come home O YE CHILDREN OF EARTH ere the great day of sorrow!

I am thy older Brother and thy Sibor Sanat Kumara..

Recorded by Sister Thedra

Sananda speaking to Sorea Sorea--

This group will grow in number and in value to the Hierarchy--many new ones will be brought into it in many ways ye know not of--- Be ye faithful to thy tasks, each as they are called will have their own work to do - and none will be more important to the work than another- all shall be blest as he responds to the call given. All shall have their reward.

Be ye not wasteful of the time- for it is short- thou hast played by the wayside to long - and now thou shall double thy diligence- and waste not a moment - lest ye be left behind - there is no time to be spent on the laggards.

Ye are not infants - ye have long walked in this way and ye can choose the way ye shall go-- Ye may stay behind with the babes in understanding who have no choice because they lack the long ages of experience in this way of light--- They have walked in darkness and cannot see the light - it is so blinding to them who are accustomed to darkness---

So many will be left in their darkness of despair - and SUCH SORROW. Be ye not one of these- BE YE NOT ONE OF THESE!

Ye who have the light would find the darkness much more agonizing. These words are not for ye few who are of this group - but for all who are walking with thee in a light which will become much brighter as ye persist- and fall not along the way.

PERSIST- and TARRY NOT!

I am thy Brother and thy Sibor Sananda

REMEMBER WHAT HAS BEEN SAID

Beloved of my being- Be ye blest of Me and of My presence- I come that ye may be blest- I give unto thee power and the authority to say unto them in my name that they shall be as ones brought out of bondage- and they shall walk in the way set before them- with great JOY and DIGNITY shall they walk- and they shall faint not- nor shall they weary of well doing- for it is near time when great trials and temptations shall beset all the peoples of the Earth- ye shall not be alone in thy trials and in thy longings--

I say unto thee thy longings shall be great indeed- and shall ye not find thy strength within thy being- which is thy eternal being- which is thyself UNVEILED-- Be ye as one which can hold fast unto the LIGHT of the CHRIST-- which never fails-- and I say unto thee ye shall find strength and peace which ye have not remembered-- Bear in mind that which has been said unto thee- and ye shall find the strength which will surpass all thy knowing- BLEST are they which hold fast in the time of trials and temptations--

I say ye shall be as ones alert- and watchful- for too I say- ONES do walk among thee which would torment thee- and take from thee thy PEACE of mind. I say unto thee-- hold fast unto the law- walk ye in the way set before thee- and ye shall find strength therein and ye shall be given the comprehension of the saints- which now walk among thee---

I say that thy martyred Saints are now within physical form- they do walk among thee- veiled though they be-- I say the ones ye have called great- and near great- the ones which have suffered that ye may follow in the path which they have found that ye might live in the temples they have founded-- that ye might have the laws revealed that ye may be brought out of bondage---.

I say unto thee these are now within physical bodies-- and they are prepared to reveal themselves unto the just and the prudent-- I say ye shall prepare thyself for great revelation- and too I say ye shall receive as ye are prepared- so be it and Selah---.

I am with thee that ye may be enlightened of God the Father- so be it My part to give unto thee as ye are prepared to receive---.

I Am thy Sibor and thy Brother Sanat Kumara---

Recorded by Sister Thedra-

SIBOR/MASTER DISCIPLE

Bor speaking- Beloved of My being- I come at this time that I might bear witness of thy integrity- I say unto thee thy hands are clean- thy heart is pure- I say unto thee: ye have been true unto thyself- ye have kept thy own counsel- ye have gone the long way to bless them- ye have given unto them that which is for them- and kept for thyself that which is given unto thee---.

I say ye have been faithful in all things and ye shall be as one which has proven thyself trust worthy- and ye shall go out from the place wherein ye are as one prepared for the greater part--.

Now I shall speak unto them which are fortuned to read these my words- There are many called and few are chosen- and they which are chosen are chosen as ones which have qualified themself through the ages past- they have labored long for their reward and they have earned the right to call themself "SIBOR" "MASTER" and "DISCIPLE"-- They qualified for each part---.

I say that even the disciple prepares himself to become a disciple of the Masters-- he has given himself-- he has brought his hands- his heart- and surrendered up himself for that which the MASTER has given unto him.

In like manner does the MASTER surrender up himself unto his SIBOR and so on-- He has the will to learn of his instructors- he has the mind- and he does not speak spiteful- nor does he cast suspicion upon his so called 'instructor'-- he gives his love and his attention-- he has been prepared for the part of DISCIPLE-

And now I say with my Brothers-- that as ye are prepared so shall ye receive- ye shall choose this day-- that which ye shall do-- and when it is come that ONE shall walk among thee as ONE prepared to give unto thee the 'WATER of LIFE'- I <u>PRAY</u> that ye may be prepared to receive HIM and of HIM--.

I say this is thy own preparation- and the law has been set before thee- ye have been fortuned this part- this knowledge- and ye have the gift of FREE WILL- and ye shall either accept or reject it--.

But let it be recorded that when it is given unto thee freely and it is rejected ye shall begin at the beginning- I say sad is the one which does be tray himself- PITY IS HE!

Blest is he which does receive of the Water of Life for he shall be forever free- So be it and Selah. I am come that ye might be alert and that ye might see and hear-- that ye may KNOW- and ye have to be thy own judge which is the way ye shall choose- none shall trespass on thy FREE WILL--.

I speak unto thee frankly and fearlessly- and I am responsible for that which I say- and none shall suffer for that which I say- and none shall suffer for that which I have said or done- I am not of a mind to see My Sibets suffer for my sake-

Yet I have said things for thy own sake- which should alert thee-- I am the Father of DISIPLINE- so be it that I am thy Brother sent of the Father and the Mother Eternal.

I Am Bor

THE GATE IS GUARDED WELL

Blest art thou this day- and blest shall ye be- for I come that this day shall bear fruit - I give unto thee of myself that ye may be blest as I have been blest of the Father Mother God- and ye shall come to know me even as I know the Father Mother---

My dear Children- for thy chidings art thou stronger- and WISER shall ye become---

I say unto thee I am not of a mind to sibor the wanton and the willful- yet I shall plant thy feet upon a hill-- I shall place within thy hand a key- which ye shall turn at will- and ye shall be as one prepared to enter into the temple gate---

I say unto thee- the gate is guarded well- and the gate stands threefold-- and the temple is foursquare-- and ye shall find the center thereof and mark it well- for there in shall be thy abiding place- Ye shall put out thy hand and I shall touch thee- and I shall quicken thee- and ye shall remember that which ye have done and said in the days of thy forgetting---

I say ye shall remember all that which ye have forgotten- such is wisdom-- I say the temple is sealed - and now it shall be unsealed and ye shall stand as ones unveiled-- thy front-piece shall be removed- and ye shall be unbound- and ye shall stand forever free and ye shall be glad- so be it and SELAH---

Praise the Father mother which has sent thee out as themself- ye are ONE with them-- only in thy unknowing have ye separated thyself from them--and ye have had thy memory blanked from thee-yet- I say ye shall have it returned unto thee- such is the WILL of the Father Mother God- so be it and Selah--

I am thy Older Brother- and thy Sibor- Sanat Kumara- so be it and Selah.

Recorded by Sister Thedra

THE CALL GOES OUT SORI SORI SORI

Blest be ye this day for I am with thee- OH, My Children- ye are blest as none other -- thine is a part different from all others-- in no age have they had that which is for tuned unto thee---

OH, My Children lift up thy hearts- raise up thy heads-- HEAR ME! HEAR YE ME!

I speak unto thee from the depth and from the heights-- I CRY unto thee--OH YE CHILDREN OF ALL THE LANDS OF THE EARTH HEAR ME!

I come that ye may <u>not</u> go down into utter darkness-- OH, YE MY BELOVED CHILDREN- long have I waited this day-- I say unto thee this is the day for which I have waited- that ye might return unto me-- be ye as ones which have ears to hear me - and a mind to learn-- and give unto me thy hand and no harm shall come near unto thee---

I say - I shall bring thee out of bondage forever- and no darkness shall consume thee-- My Children I have said unto thee at this altar-that I shall bring thee out as ye are prepared- so be it and I ask of the ought- that ye may learn of me-- it is necessary to give unto me thy heart- thy hand - and surrender up thyself- for all thy opinions shall avail thee naught-- I say ye shall come unto me void of thy preconceived ideas- and void of opinions-- I say ye know me not! And ye can find me in the temple wherein ye shall come- I say within the place wherein I am ye shall find me ready to receive - and I shall welcome thee home

I say unto thee My Children- of ALL the Lands of the EARTH- I have not turned thee away-- ye have forgotten me--long have ye gone from me- and ye have not had the mind to return unto me-- I say unto thee ye shall not give thought unto me-- and ye shall ponder my words- and I shall reveal myself unto thee- and ye shall be glad! Great shall be thy revelations- and GREAT shall be thy JOY!

I am with thee and I am GLAD! so be it I shall watch thy progress and I shall speak unto thee many times--and ye which are of a mind shall receive me- in the name of the MOST HIGH LIVING GOD- so be it and Selah

I am thy Mother Eternal--Sarah.

Recorded by Sister Thedra

THE ONE TO COME: MOTHER SARAH

Sori Sori Sori-- Sarah speaking -- Beloved Child which is my hand made manifest unto them- blest art thou- and blest shall ye be---

Be ye as my voice unto them and say unto them in my name - and as I would have thee say- that one shall come unto thee from out the great cosmos-- from out the heart of God the Father shall he come-- and he shall take upon him a body of flesh- a body of flesh and bone - and he shall be as one come for the first time---

I say he has not had the body of flesh and bone--he has not gone into darkness--nor shall he-- for he shall be as one sent of the Father- and he shall not have his memory blanked from him- for he shall remember all that HE IS- and all that He shall ever BE-- He shall know -- he shall walk among thee as one prepared for this day---

He shall walk as one which has all power- and as one prepared to give unto them, as the Father made incarnate upon the earth--- I say great is this day- and Great IS this Day!

I say the heavens shall open up its doors- and they which are so prepared shall have free concourse into all the places thereof---

I say ye shall prepare thyself - for that which is yet to come- I say ye shall be as ONES prepared for that which shall come upon the earth- too- I say ye shall see the fulfillment of all the prophecies which have been given for this time - for there shall be GREAT and trying times--- When the waters shall flow upward- and the fire shall mingle with the water--and the thorn shall grow on the wheat--and the rose shall bloom from the oak---

I say ye shall live to see prophecy fulfilled--and for this shall ye prepare thyself --- Ye shall bless this day when ye have received me- and of me-- for I shall send one out from the place of my abode-which shall gather them in which are so prepared-- and they shall be gathered as the hen gathers her chicks---

Be ye as one on whose shoulders rests the responsibility of that which shall be given unto thee to do-- I say each shall play his part - and for this shall be prepare himself, and ye shall not fall- nor shall ye falter - for I say unto thee - I SHALL WALK WITH THEE AND I SHALL SUSTAIN THEE---

PEARLS ARE MY CHILDREN-- and JEWELS are my thoughts--

And few are prepared to receive my JEWELS---

And not one of MY PEARLS shall go unaccounted for- for they are numbered - ONE by ONE-- I know each by name- and I see them whereever they be- and I have suckled them at my breast- and I hold them close that they may not go in deep sleep--I nourish them - and I give unto them as they are prepared to receive--I say I do not waste time or energy in vain - I am the Mother eternal- and I know them which sleepeth- and them which are awake--and I too know them which are beginning to stir from their slumbers---

Now it is come when many shall awaken- and they shall be glad it is over--for it is given unto me to know that which has bound them in the hours of their unknowing - in the time of their sleep---

Now they shall call out and they shall be heard and answered - and they shall be blest indeed- and they shall be brought in and refreshed and purified- such is the will of the Father---

I ask of thee nothing more than accept my love and my hand - and I shall bring thee into the place wherein I am- and I shall rejoice with thee that it is finished---

Praise the name of Solen forever and forever for he has given unto thee being - and he has given of himself that ye might be-- and he has willed that ye return unto him this day- so be it and I am thy Mother Eternal- Sarah-

Recorded by Sister Thedra

THE EMERALD CROSS

THE CROSS IS A COMPANY--AN ORDER OF BEINGS WHO WORK WITHIN THE BROTHERHOOD OF MAN AND THE FATHERHOOD OF GOD--FOR THE GOOD OF ALL MANKIND---

AND AT THE HEAD OF THIS GROUP ONE KNOWN AS MOTHER SARAH, THE PERSONIFICATION OF LOVE - EMBODIMENT OF ALL MOTHERS. -THAT IS: THE LOVE OF GOD THE FATHER MADE <u>MANIFEST IN MOTHERS</u>-- THE BLESSED MOTHER SARAH IS THE HEAD OF THIS ORDER OF THE EMERALD CROSS---

AND WHEN ONE EARNS THE DIVINE RIGHT AND PRIVILEGES TO ASSOCIATE THEMSELF WITH THIS ORDER IT IS THE JOY OF ALL THE ORDERS- AND

BROTHERS OF LIGHT-- I SPEAK FOR THE ORDER- FOR I AM ONE KNOWN AS MERSEDA.

SPOKEN TO SISTER THEDRA OF THE EMERALD CROSS.

Born speaking:

I speak unto thee from out the emanations of deity-- I speak unto thee from the fullness of eternity-- I call unto thee from the depth from the heights--

I speak of SPIRIT-- I speak of flesh-- I speak of that which eternally is- and that which changeth not--

I speak unto thee of that which shall- and does change-- I speak of CHANGE- and change is GOOD; and shall be good ---

And no man shall stay the hand of DEITY--- I say; NO MAN SHALL CHANGE THE LAW for it the law that all things within the realm of matter be changed---

There is no staleness within the realm of spirit; spirit is the newness of all things made pure--- -

I say: All things which are within the realm of matter shall be changed; cleansed and made pure, such is the law---I say; such is the law of the GREAT and GRAND SPIRIT - Father Mother God- which has called forth all manifestation- which is made manifest---

I say; all that is now made manifest shall be returned unto SPIRIT and made fresh- made pure---

I say it is the law which is given unto all the lands- all the countries- all planets- all galaxies- all peoples within and on all planets- all galaxies throughout the systems of all creation, all that which is created and that which shall be created---

Now ye shall speak unto them in my name; and as I would- that- I come unto them from out the heart of God the Father---

I come as HIS emanation that He has willed; that He has sent out as His pulsation-- as his breath- And I would speak unto thee as a Brother which as yet- has not taken upon SELF the body of flesh and bone---

I have not spoken as man-- I have not spoken as one of earth-- I have not been born of woman-- YET - I AM-- I am unborn of earth-- yet I shall take embodiment through woman upon earth---

As earth shall I be born -- I say; unto thee; I shall be born of woman - in the same manner as was thy Lord- known into thee was Jesus the Christ- known unto us as Sananda Son of God ---

I say - in like manner shall I be born-- I say one has been prepared as was the mother Mary- of Jesus thy Lord- the Master Sananda---

I say one has been prepared even as she; that she may receive me-- as a child of twelve I shall make my entrance into the world of man- and therein shall I walk and talk---

I shall bring with me a legion of the realms of light-- I shall have a place prepared for to receive me- and I shall have a place within the land wherein ye are at this time: I say the place is there; and it is now being prepared-- and it is guarded well --- And I say there are great preparations being made to receive me-- and the hosts which I shall bring with me --- And when I shall go out I shall be as no man has been--I shall be different from all others-- I say I shall be different from all others---

I shall carry with me a blue star and all which looks upon it shall know me, and they shall be gathered into the place wherein I am- wherein I shall be at that place, wherein I shall abide- and they shall become part of the host which I shall have with me---

I say ye shall prepare thyself- for ye know not that which is to be- that which shall come upon the earth--- I say great revelation is in store for thee; and great shall be the day ahead--- Blest shall ye be- and blest art thou-- Blest shall they be which endureth to the end.

I am BORN--

Recorded by Thedra

Sanat Kumara speaking:

Be ye blest of me and by me- for I come that ye may be blest--- Ye have given unto me great joy- for ye have overcome that which has been unto thee a great and heavy cross: ye have been true unto thyself; and ye have held thy peace- and ye have given unto thyself credit for knowing which way to go-- ye have gone the way set before thee-- ye have given of thyself that they may be blest-- ye have faltered not - nor have ye stumbled-- I say ye have done well.

I say ye shall be blest- so be it and Selah.

Now let it be recorded that there shall be a mighty wind and it shall be unto they place of abode--- Many there shall be which shall look for a place to lay their head and they shall be given the place - and they shall be as ones which have with them the children which shall be comforted in the time of stress- so be it and SELAH.

I say ye shall comfort them in the time of stress-- such is my word unto thee-- for I have spoken and ye have heard me- so be it and Selah.

I am thy older Brother Sanat Kumara

The following is Sananda's answer to a letter received at this altar:--

***

Beloved: I speak unto thee as one which has my hand upon thee, and I say ye shall be blest of me and by me: and I say ye shall speak unto this one... as I would - and ye shall speak as I would in LOVE- for I AM LOVE- I move in the SPIRIT of LOVE- I say: I AM LOVE IN ACTION I say I AM come that ALL MEN may come to know me- and as they receive me- so shall they receive the Father.

I say: I AM COME-- I walk in thy midst- and I speak unto them which have prepared themself for to receive me.

I go not into the places of the Dragon for entertainment--- I play a lone hand! I am not deceived by appearances! I am not deceived by words- for I KNOW what prompts them! I am not DECEIVED by ANYTHING-- for I am not a FOOL- neither do I sibor FOOLS-- I speak fearlessly- and wisely-- I speak out of compassion for the FOOLISH-- for they are as the little ones- they know not how short the time left for their preparation-- I say- LIFE is LIFE! No beginning, No end.

Ye shall REMEMBER this: "NO END." DEATH IS AN ILLUSION: NO ESCAPE FROM THE LAW! As ye set it into motion it shall fill its cycle and return-- ALL thy Joy- all thy TORMENT! Pity- are they which set into motion that which shall torment them: I say they betray themself- they shall be as ones which have thrown overboard their own life-belt! So be it I have spoken and I AM NOT FINISHED!

I Am thy Master, Thy Sibor, thy Brother which has gone before thee to prepare the way- so be ye wise to walk in it -- I am the Nazerine Sananda- Jesus Christ.

Sister Thedra Recorder

Each Unto His Own Part -The Hundred and Forty Four

Sarah Speaking...

Beloved of my being -- blest are thou and blest shall ye be --

Ye have gone out from me as one which has gone into the earth for a part which is thine. All which are within the earth at this time have certain parts -- each unto his own and no two are equal - alike - for it is as thy fingerprints -- no two alike. And for the first time I speak unto thee on this subject - and it is for thee to give unto them which are of a mind to learn.

I say give this unto them which are of a mind to learn. There are many within the earth at this time which have parts in the great and divine plan -- and no two are alike for they are "parts" -- no one has the whole part -- and each unto his own.

I say each has been given a part and many have not as yet awakened unto his part -- and too, let it go on record that each is prepared for his part from the beginning of his going out -- yet some sleep and are as the traitor-- he betrays himself -- he thinks himself <u>wise</u> and he turns from his appointed course; for this does he pay the price. I say he pays a pretty price -- he ransoms himself - from his own prison - he ransoms himself from the self-created hell - he ransoms himself from his own bondage.

Poor in spirit is he which turns aside from his appointed course. Now when they which go out as ones called from the hierarchy they are given "parts" and <u>entrusted</u> with certain parts, and as they prepare themself there are greater parts entrusted them.

And when they have been found worthy they are brought into the place where in there are treasures untold; wherein they sit in council as "one" and wherein there is a hundred and forty four of the learned - which are of the Royal Assembly, and these which make up this council are as the ones which have thy records; and nothing is overlooked, nothing hidden - and no one is judge of another -- the record is the judge. I say they which are called shall answer and they shall stand before this tribunal as the initiate which has prepared himself for this part.

Now it is come when one from among thee shall walk among thee and he shall find them which are prepared to be brought in before the Royal Assembly, and they which are brought in shall be as ones which have prepared themself in advance.

I say the path is narrow and straight. I say ye have the key unto the gate - be ye as ones prepared for the greater part -- praise ye the Lord of Hosts for mighty is his name -- praise ye his name all ye people of the earth.

I am thy eternal mother, Sarah.

Recorded by Sister Thedra of the Emerald Cross

The Condition Known as "Sleep"

Sanat Kumara speaking unto thee of a condition known unto us as sleep. When one is in lethargy he sleeps for a time and awakens within the body of flesh refreshed from his labors. And when he has refreshed himself he has a clear mind and a poised body. And when he has a poised body and a clear mind he is receptive to the greater learning - to revelation.

And he is as one of a mind to learn -- he has the will to learn. When he is asleep he neither has the mind or the will. Hence we refer to them as the "sleepers" -- they belong to the sleepers' realm. I say they are asleep! And they have not the mind to learn, nor the will.

Such is the mind of many which are as ones which go and come in the world of man. I say they are of the sleepers' realm and they care not to awaken. And too, I say - should the Lord and master Jesus Christ Sananda Son of God walk among them this day and speak unto them as he does speak unto thee and unto all his servants which do serve him on their behalf -- they would crucify him this day -- they would spit upon him -- and they would think upon new ways to torture him. I say the mind of the beast is in them. I say they are not as ones prepared to receive him. And surely not prepared for the inmost place of the Most High Living God.

Ye shall say unto them in my name and with the authority which is mine: I am now prepared to come out from the place wherein I am as one fully qualified to give unto them as they are prepared to receive. I say as they are prepared so shall they receive.

I am not so foolish as to waste my energy on the foolish - for I have spoken for lo these many days that it is now time to be at thy posts of duty - up and about thy Father's business - and I find them as ones forcing upon others their own will - their own parts - their own puny words which they have pilfered from yet others.

I say they know not that the Day of the "Lord" has come. I say they are to be found prattling as babes. They are to be found in the places of gaming - wherein they indulge their senses of pleasure. They seek pleasure - not wisdom.

I say they seek phenomenon - not truth - they are blind as the male mole. They cry for the things of earth - they wander to and fro bound as by their leg irons. They cry, Lord! Lord! and they seek him not. Such is the pity of man this day.

.I say unto thee weep not for them -- turn not neither to the right nor to the left -- but walk ye in the way which ye shall go. Be ye blest this day and the labor of thy hands shall be blest. Mighty is the name of Solen - Solen - praise him all ye children of earth - lift up thy eyes - open up thy hearts and receive of him thy eternal freedom. Blest shall ye be.

I am thy older brother, Sanat Kumara.

Recorded by Sister Thedra of the Emerald Cross

Sananda: HEAR Me! HEAR Me!

Sananda speaking -- Beloved of my being, it is now come when changes shall come about upon the earth and throughout thy country shall be much sorrow and unrest. I say that these changes shall bring unrest and much suffering. And too, I say that there are none so sad as the ones which betray themself. And in a short while ye shall see great strands of water wherein are no waters. Ye shall see the waters dry up wherein they have been. Ye shall see great pestilences rise up to torment thee -- ye shall give these words to be them: As I say them, for they shall hear that which I say and they shall not spit upon them.

For they shall live to see the day not far off when one shall place himself upon the throne which he sets up and he shall call himself God -- he shall decree that they bow unto him and pay unto him homage, and he shall demand of them human sacrifice and they shall do his bidding. Now I say ye shall hear me out: for I am not of a mind to sacrifice up my own -- I am of a mind to alert thee - yet should ye turn a deaf ear - I am helpless. I cry unto thee - Oh my children, be ye alert and hear me! I say ye shall have trying times and ye shall be as ones true unto thyself and ye shall cling unto the light. Ye shall ask of the Father light - and truth. Ask for comprehension and walk ye in the way set before thee.

I say that the way of the dragon is a subtle thing - he would deceive thee and cause thee to be befuddled - he would give unto thee the bitter cup -- he would divide my sheep and scatter them. My children! My children which I call my sheep, I say he would scatter thee - and confuse thee. I say unto thee be ye as one which has my hand upon thee and ye shall be led out of bondage - out of darkness, such is my word unto thee. Hold fast unto the law set before thee and glad shall ye be.

I am thy sibor and thy brother, Sananda, son of God. So be it and Selah.

"Grieve not for those who fall on the field of service--for theirs is a crown of Glory....

"Know ye not that there are martyred Saints that walk among you UNCROWNED?

"I am come that ye may have the comprehension to recognize them. Were it not for them I would bring thee into the place wherein I am thru levitation--it will be done--thru a closed circle -- "

Recorded by Sister Thedra of the Emerald Cross

The Dragon is Bound in His Own Den

Sananda speaking -- Beloved of my being, my hand is and has been upon thee; I say I am with thee and I shall not forsake thee. I say I am not of a mind to forsake thee and I am given unto watchfulness.

I see that which goes on about thee. I say unto thee the lash of the dragon's tail is but the ill wind which bloweth the stench from out his nostrils; he has been bound and he has his hands tied and he has no power to touch thee -- and he is now incarcerated within his own den -- and he is furious he has no power over thee -- for from this day forward shall he be bound -- he shall not come near unto thee. This is my word - my promise unto thee, my child -- dry thy tears and give unto me credit for that which I am -- and I say unto thee I am the keeper at the gate - I am thy gate keeper and I see that no unclean thing enter into this port - I come into this port and I shall keep it clean that I might use it for the good of all mankind - so shall it be.

Be ye as one prepared for the greater part and ye shall be glad, so be it a time of rejoicing. Amen, so be it, and Selah.

Say unto them which is called Unit No. 3 that a unit such as they shall stand as "One," with "one mind," "one purpose," and they shall be as one which has the mind to serve the will of the Father -- and they shall be as ones ready for that which shall be given unto them to do. They shall be as ones prepared at all times to be called at the midnight hour. For in the time which is near there shall be a great voice ring out thru the cosmos. And it shall be recognized by all which has alerted themself and prepared themself for this day.

I say they which are asleep shall be as the sleepers; they shall be found dreaming - and their dreams shall torment them and they shall be as ones confused and they shall be as ones frightened and without solace.

I say they which are of a mind to learn and which are of a mind to follow me shall be alert and they shall be without confusion and they shall be as ones which have my hand upon them and I shall lead them with surety and they shall not fall - nor shall they stumble - I say they shall not stumble and fall - for I am of the Father sent and I am not of a mind to leave my sheep unto the wolves.

Blest are they which hold fast unto the law and blest shall they be. I am come that my sheep be not scattered - yet they hear the voices of strange masters which they would follow in the time of their confusion. I say they are as ones frightened and confused - for the day of sifting is at hand - and they call out in their delirium and they are as ones bound by that which they know not. They have not the power within their own hand to fight off the beast - they have not the wisdom which is of the Christed ones - that which is of the Father - without their knowing they have naught, I say they have naught. So be it and Selah.

To <u>know</u> is wisdom - to <u>think</u> is uncertainty and to think is not to know. I say therein lies the difference between belief and wisdom. Man's opinions is not the mind of the Father -- and it is the tower of Babel which shall fall. It shall crumble at their feet -- For they which <u>think</u> themselves wise shall be found wanting. I say they shall be brought face to face with their foolishness -- so be it and Selah.

I am responsible for that which I say and no man shall call me a fool -- so be it and Selah. I am Sananda, son of God.

* * * * * *

The One to Come Shall Take Upon Himself The Cross of Flesh

Sanat Kumara Speaking -- Beloved of my being -- be ye as my mouth and as my hand made manifest unto the ones which gather themself together, and say unto them in my name that it is now come when great shall be the activities within the earth and about it.

I say we which do sit in council are alert -- we have our eyes open and we see and know that which does go on, and I say with wisdom and with surety that it is the part of thy guardians to protect thee in the hours of stress. I say that there are no traitors among us -- we speak unto truth and wisdom and we speak fearlessly for it is given unto us to know the law. And I say we abide by it, so be it that we walk in the way which we point out unto thee, and I say that we have gone before thee to prepare the way before thee. And ye shall prepare thyself diligently for that which shall be entrusted unto thee to do.

Now let this go on record that each has his own free will and none shall trespass upon it. And when one comes unto thee and inquires of thee ye shall give unto him the law and he shall choose that which he shall do with it. He shall be as one free to choose -- he shall be as one wise to choose to abide by it -- he shall be as a traitor unto himself to refuse it. So be it the law as they ask so shall they receive -- so be it and Selah.

I say one shall come from out the east and he shall be as no other, and he shall be as one which has taken embodiment through woman, yet he shall be of light - he shall not be the seed of man, and he shall go out from his place of physical birth at the age of twelve and he shall walk among thee as God the Father made manifest in flesh.

He has not been born of woman (before); he has not walked the earth as man -- and he has not taken upon himself the cross of flesh. I say he has not taken upon himself the chemical form of animal man. He has not come into thy realm (before). He shall -- and ye shall be as ones to see him - I say he shall bring great light and all which are so prepared shall walk with him and see him face to face - such shall be thy reward -- So be it and Selah.

I am thy brother and thy sibor, Sanat Kumara.

Recorded by Sister Thedra of the Emerald Cross

As the Moth Which Goes Into The Flame

Beloved of my being: Ye have said that which I have given unto thee to say. And I speak unto thee as one prepared to give unto thee the "new" part. And it shall be new - separate - and unlike any other.

Ye shall be as one prepared for this part. And I say unto thee the "old" shall serve thee well. And ye shall bless the day which has been unto thee thy stepping stone. Ye have gone the long way to bless them and they have not known thee. Nor are they of a mind to recognize thee.

I say they shall be as ones awakened unto the Father's work. And they shall be as ones come alive. I say they shall awaken and they shall come alive. I say they which have my hand upon them shall awaken. I am not so foolish as to awaken them aforehand, for it is not lawful. They should be as the moth which goes into the flame -- they should be as the cocoon which is opened afore time. I am not unmindful of the law.

I say: I am mindful of my sheep and one which is qualified to do the Father's will -- thru me it is done. So be it and Selah.

Blest shall ye be this day. Blest shall they be which comes unto this altar.

Be they blest of me. I am Sananda, Son of God.

Recorded by Sister Thedra of the Emerald Cross

BORN - THE VIRGIN SPIRIT

Boran

Sori - Sori - Sori -- Be ye blest of me and by me. I come unto thee from out the great cosmic heart. I bring unto thee great tidings. I bless thee with such tidings that I bring. I say unto thee: be ye mindful of that which I am saying unto thee at this time.

The day is now come when one shall walk upon the earth in flesh as Spirit made manifest - which is from out the heart of the cosmos, from out the heart of all divinity - And he shall be as God the Father incarnate in flesh. He shall be a virgin spirit - for he has not taken upon himself a body of flesh and bone - he has not walked among man as such - he has not been as one which has gone out from the Father. He has not in any form separated himself from the Father. And he shall now go out as man -- for the first time shall he go out.

I say: He shall take upon himself the garment of flesh and bone - he shall walk as man - he shall be as man, yet he shall be as none other - for he shall be as God incarnate -- he shall be as the living, breathing pulsating life of God the Father. He shall know himself to be the Father incarnate. And he shall go into a place which is prepared to receive him. And he shall take upon himself a body of earthly substance thru woman. I say: he shall be born of the womb of woman. He shall be the fruit of woman yet he shall not be the seed of man - for he shall be born of God the Father. He shall be of light. He shall be as one which has not gone into darkness. I say: He shall be no part of darkness. He shall be as one which is the perfect man - he shall be as none other - he shall be born within the land which is called the greatest of all nations. He shall be as one filled with wisdom and all power shall be his - for he knoweth all things. And he has the form of man - yet he will be prepared to change it at will.

Such shall be his knowledge and he shall be master of all law and all things. I say unto thee - ye which have ears to hear and eyes to see - be ye as ones alert and ye shall be given much which has not hitherto been revealed unto thee lo the eons of time ye have waited.

I say: Ye have awaited this day when earth should receive her King. Be ye blest this day and blest shall ye be. I am come unto thee this day that ye may be prepared for the greater part. I am thy brother and thy sibor, Boran,

Recorded by Sister Thedra of the Emerald Cross

The King of Glory --

"He shall come in as a mighty sound - as a mighty trumpet.."

Berean

Berean speaking unto thee: This day shall I speak unto thee concerning the coming of the King. Ye have been told that the King of Glory shall make his appearance in the time which is near. It is true. So be it.

I come unto thee from out the cosmic center of light, I speak in all languages. I have spoken all languages and I shall, for it is now come when many shall speak unto the earth children. As man shall they speak and in the languages which each people can understand. I say each shall be spoken unto in his own language that he may understand that which is said unto him.

I say we which are of the hierarchy do speak as we do for a purpose. I say it is given in a certain manner for a purpose. And that purpose is not a mystery, for it is the greater part of wisdom. And when ye have gone the way of the initiate it shall be revealed unto thee.

I say ye are an '<u>impatient</u> people' filled with curiosity and wonderment. Ye are <u>not patient</u> and kind. Ye rush and push thy way into the halls of learning. Ye try to absorb thy knowledge from books. Ye search the scripts and ye look for signs, and for confirmation. Ye look for peace and security - ye find none! Ye are as ones which have been following man. Ye seek after signs and miracles. Ye are as little children chasing bubbles. I say ye shall now grow to the age of maturity and ye shall be given as ye are prepared to receive. I say ye shall engrave upon thy heart that which is said unto thee. And ye shall remember it. For in the days ahead all things shall pass away and all thy knowledge of these things swept with them. Ye have nothing! Ye have nothing!

And thy security is as naught. I speak as one which sees and knows. I know for I am one with the Father which has given unto me being and he has not withheld his wisdom from me. I say ye shall stand shorn of all thy credentials - of all thy passports - of all thy glory - of all thy wealth which ye have clung to so tenaciously. Ye shall stand naked - ye shall stand naked!

Ye shall be as ones wealthy indeed which do enrich thy own life with that which we bring. I say ye shall be as ones rich indeed when ye make of thyself "A son of God" -- Ye shall walk as a son of God the Father. Ye shall walk upright. Ye shall give of thyself that others might be comforted. Ye shall be a lamp unto their feet. Ye shall heed these my words -- mark them well -- and engrave them upon thy heart -- and they shall not depart from thee.

I say ye shall listen for the trumpet which shall ring out. It shall sound thruout all the cosmos. And ye shall awaken as from the dead. Ye shall lift up thy eyes. And ye shall behold the King of Glory, for he shall come in as a mighty sound - as a mighty trumpet - he shall come as a great light. He shall come as a mighty host, for he shall be as one which has not been seen -- he <u>shall</u> be seen!

And they which are not prepared for this day shall fall upon their face and call out Lord! Lord! They shall freeze in their tracks from fright. They shall die of heart failure. They shall run unto a hiding place. They shall panic! And I say unto thee - they shall be as ones gone mad.

Ye shall be as ones prepared for this day, for it is not afar off -- it has been said that the anti-Christ is now upon earth in flesh and bone. It is so -- so be it!

We sleepeth not - nor are we unmindful of our children -- we are as parents - watchful of the little ones. We do not tarry with the trivialities. We are about the Father's business. Such is wisdom.

I speak unto thee from out the center of the Cosmos that ye may have light. I shall speak unto thee again and again. Be ye blest of me and by me. I am Berean.

Recorded by Sister Thedra of the Emerald Cross

Sanat Kumara..."Ye are the microcosm of His being...

Sanat Kumara speaking. Be ye as ones blest this day. For from the One I come unto thee as deity personified in me. I say I come as one sent of God the Father that ye may be blest. I say unto thee that one shall walk among thee as man and he shall be as one sent of God the

Father. He shall come in the time which is near and he shall bring with him a mighty host. For he shall come as one of light. For it is now come when balance shall be established within the earth. It shall be established in the firmaments -- it shall be established within thee -- for ye are as the microcosm -- ye are the breath of the Father -- Ye are his breath -- Ye are the microcosm -- Ye are but the microcosm of his being. Ye are but his breath crystalized into form - each form which ye have taken - and ye are of no part of the nether world. Ye are eternally of Him the Father which has given unto thee being.

Ye are his hand and his foot made manifest upon the earth. I say unto thee be ye as ones which can comprehend that which I say unto thee. Ye are His hand and His foot -- for none other has he - he has created and that creation shall and does serve him as thy hand and as thy foot serves thee.

I say he has no other hand and foot except that which he creates. He creates as he sees fit. And he cuts off as he sees fit. I say he casts off that which he creates for he has within his hand the power to cast off or to create anew. He has the One and Only power -- he has the power to give - the power to take. He has the love and wisdom of the Father, and none other has the right to cast off or to take on. For he has gone out he has not gone out - he has remained ever the same - and yet he is change -- ever changeless - yet all changing. Ye have not the comprehension of his nature at this time. The greatness is beyond thy concept, yet ye shall know, for ye shall come to know the boundlessness of his love and his mercy. Ye shall be as he for ye shall be enfolded in his bosom -- Ye shall be embraced in his hands - he shall enfold thee within his bosom. He shall hold thee unto himself and he shall be glad. I say ye shall come to know him, the

Father, for it is willed by him that ye return unto him and be made whole. So be it and Selah.

So be it, and so be it, I am with thee this day and I am glad. I come that ye may return unto the place of thy going out. And it shall be a great day. There shall be much rejoicing and great gladness. So be it and Selah.

I am Sanat Kumara.

Recorded by Sister Thedra of the Emerald Cross

Anti-Christs

Sori - Sori - Sori -- Blest of the Father art thou - blest of me art thou. I come of the Father. I am of the Father sent that they may have this portion which shall be given unto thee for them. Ye shall give it unto them and they shall accept it in the name of the Father, Son and Holy Ghost. Amen and Selah.

I am he which was called "The Wayshower" - yet they which proclaim me know me not - them which know me follow me. I say they which do no more than proclaim me know me not. I, too, say they which have their hand in mine look not to the left nor to the right -- they walk which way I point -- they argue not the point.

Such are the blind and the deaf -- they see not the way when I point -- they hear not that which I say -- yet they babble on. I say they cannot find me in books nor can they find me asleep. For it is now come when great shall be the activity within the earth and I say great shall be the activity within the realms of light. I say that the shepherds are not asleep - they know each and every lamb. They know the wolves and their hiding places. I say they lie in wait for the unsuspecting -- they lie in wait to ensnare thee. They are cunning and cruel, for they are the anti-Christs.

I say the anti-Christs are among thee and they seek out the ones which are of a mind to be used by them -- they would silence thy voice and tie thy hands. And they would torment thee. I say ye shall be alert and ye shall be as one about thy preparation. For it is now come when ye shall choose which way ye shall go. I am come that ye might choose wisely. I Am. And I know myself to be Son of God the Father known as Solen the First and the Last. I am Sananda.

* * * * *

Sananda
There are none without the presence of God. Yet few know that presence. And it is said without that knowing ye have nothing. I say again: Without thy knowing, ye have nothing. Ye are as ones impoverished. And ye are as ones bound and ye know not by which ye are bound. Ye are of the dark in thy blindness.

I come that ye may be made to see -- and to know -- and by my grace shall ye see. I say I shall raise up my hand and ye shall be caused to see. I say I shall speak and ye shall hear. I say ye shall will it so - and so be it.

I am now prepared to step forth and give unto thee as I have received of the Father which has sent me. I come unto thee in his name -- and I bless thee as he would have me bless thee. Be ye as ones blest. Accept that which I offer thee in his name, and by him through me shall ye be brought out of bondage.

Be ye at peace and poise. Give unto no man credit for taking it from thee. Adoni Adomni and Sheloheim Adomni.

Recorded by Sister Thedra of the Emerald Cross

Sananda-- "Ye are of the specie which have the brow which shall carry the star..."

Sori - Sori - Sori. Beloved children, be ye blest this day, and blest shall ye be. I come to thee that ye shall walk in the way set before thee -- ye shall be as one which has my hand upon thee and ye shall not fall nor shall ye stumble. I say when ye are of a mind to be led I shall lead thee gladly and I shall give of myself that ye may not stumble. I give of my strength, my energy, my love, my wisdom - for I am of the Father sent that ye may know even as I know.

Yet, my children, I say unto thee again I am as one helpless to give unto thee before ye have prepared thyself to receive of me and by me. Ye have within thy own hand the power to reach out and take that which I have - yet I shall have no less. I say ye have within thy hand the power to reach out and take that which I have and I should not be impoverished thereby.

I am now prepared to give unto thee as I have received of God the Father. For this has he sent me. And ye which are as ones bound by conventions, dogmas, creeds and within thy own opinions - ye are as ones which close me out. Ye simply close me out. I stand and knock, and ye hear me do it not. I call and ye answer me not.

I speak gently while ye are sleeping and ye hear me not. I cry aloud from the mountain tops. I scale the heights and place thereupon my marks, and ye are as deaf and blind. Ye recognize them not. Ye hear nothing which I say. I am now prepared to call again, and I shall use the trumpet - for it is now come when ye shall hear! I say ye shall hear - and ye shall see - and ye shall be wise indeed to prepare thyself for such as ye shall hear and see. For it is now come when great changes shall come upon the earth and upon all peoples of the earth. And woe unto them which are found wanting.

I say we are not ministers of doom. We are not born of doom. We preach deliverance. And ye are of a species which have the brow which shall carry the star and ye have the fortune to be sent from another galaxy and ye are within the earth for a part which is being enacted in the eternal scheme of evolution - and of the earth - and of man. For ye are not alone. Every planet has life of one kind or another. For this are the planets created. Such is the wisdom of the Creator.

There are ones upon the earth this day which have come from far and distant planets that this age may be brought into its fullness. I say great shall be this age. So be it and Selah. Ye have not glimpsed the glory which <u>is</u> and which <u>shall</u> <u>be</u>. I say ye shall live to see the Glory of the King! Ye shall see him and ye shall know him.

Ye shall be as one wise to prepare thyself that ye might be caught up with him. So be it and Selah.

I am thy sibor and thy brother, Sananda.

Recorded by Sister Thedra of the Emerald Cross

BORN

The Coming of the King

Sananda speaking. Beloved of my being, be ye blest of me and by me. For I come that ye may be blest. Ye shall now say unto them in my name that one shall walk among them as man and he shall be as flesh and bone. Yet he shall be the Father made manifest upon earth. He shall be as one which has not been embodied in flesh before.

I say unto thee he shall be as none other for he shall come into embodiment for the first time. His name shall be called "Born" -- and he shall be as the son of woman, yet he shall not be the seed of man. He shall be of light, and for this is he prepared to come among thee as man. He shall wear a coat of skin which shall not be unto him a burden. He shall not be bound by it.

Now ye shall say unto them that in the time which is near he shall be born in the greatest of all nations. He shall be as one cloistered until he is of the twelfth year. Then he shall go out into the world wherein he shall reign as King Supreme!

I say he shall reign as King Supreme. So be it and Selah.

Now ye shall ask, Why is this? Where is this? And ye shall be as ones curious. I say ye shall first seek wisdom and all thy questions shall be answered. So be it and Selah.

I am now prepared to speak unto thee at length concerning his coming, yet ye shall be as ones prepared for the great day when ye shall see him face to face. So be it and Selah.

I am thy sibor and thy brother, Sananda.

Recorded by Sister Thedra of the Emerald Cross

Sananda-- ...." The Power of The Word "

Sananda speaking. Beloved, my hand is upon thee and great shall be thy revelation for it is now come when great shall be the light which shall flood the earth, and the ones which are unprepared shall be as the sleepers and the traitors. They shall sleep on, and they which betray themself shall be the saddest of the lot.

Be ye as one which has the light which is - always has been - and ever shall be. And ye shall know that which is meant by Light and Truth -- and ye shall walk by it. Ye shall be unto thyself true and ye shall bless this day. And ye shall keep it holy and ye shall have no false gods before him which has given unto thee being. And ye shall praise him and ye shall be unto him all that he would have thee be. So be it ye shall glorify him in the earth and ye shall be unto him his hand and his foot made manifest upon the earth. And ye shall walk which way he sets before thee. Ye shall bless them which do speak evil against thee and ye shall love them for that which they are and not for that which they do. Praise ye the name of Solen Aum Solen Solen - the power and the radiation of that power shall go out from him thru thee. And ye shall radiate that power and vibration which that sound and vibration carries. I say it carries great power -- and it is the Word and the Word was God -- and the Word became manifest, and the manifestation was God and was good. And so be it and let it be so. I am and I know myself to be, so be it. I am Sananda Son of God the Father. Amen.

*   *   *   *

Beloved of my being - be ye blest of me and by me, and I shall come in and abide with thee. Be ye at peace and poise and say unto them that there are none so foolish as them which think themself wise. And ye shall say unto them in my name that I shall lead them which hear my voice and which have the mind to follow me. It is now come when great stress shall be upon all peoples of the earth and great shall be thy endurance.

I say ye which have the will to follow me shall be led with surety and ye shall find the strength which comes not of flesh, yet which is of flesh shall be strengthened from the peace and the poise which is not of earth. Celestial songs shall ye sing within thy heart and great shall be thy peace within a world of men gone mad. I say the world of men gone mad shall not torment thee. Look unto the heavens from whence cometh thy blessings and from whence cometh thy strength. Peace and good will for all mankind shall abide within thee and great shall be thy blessings.

I keep thee this day and I am not unmindful of that which goes on in the world of man. So be it that I am at the throne of my Father prepared to do his bidding. And I come unto thee that ye may know him as I know him. So be it and Selah.

I am thy sibor and thy brother, Sananda.

Recorded by Sister Thedra of the Emerald Cross

SORNICA

"The 144--the 12......"

Sornica speaking unto thee concerning the temple of the great white altar. I say unto thee the temple which is and which has been since the days when the sons of solitude went into the east to establish a school wherein the secrets of man - the history of man and his beginning upon earth - and his origin - might be preserved for this day - for this age.

I say it is now come when great shall be the revelation of and unto them which are prepared for such. I say that all who are found trustworthy and who have followed the law shall be brought into the temple which is - and was established by the Sons of Solitude - they are the seven which are the directors of certain activities and they are the 12 -- there are 144 in toto and these brothers are within the temple of the great white altar at this time.

And I say ye which are as ones alert and true unto thyself shall be given proof of these my words. And I have given unto thee a key and ye shall be as ones wise and keep that which I say unto thee for thyself, for it is the better part of wisdom. For in the time which is near one shall come unto thee with a plan and ye shall hear him out. So be it and Selah.

I am come that this might be said. So be it and Selah. I am thy brother, Sornica.

Recorded by Sister Thedra of the Emerald Cross

PRAYER

Sananda speaking unto thee.

Be ye blest of me and by me for I am come that ye may be blest. Ye shall give this unto them and they shall make it their own. And none shall lay claim unto it for it shall belong to the ones which hold it within their hearts and none shall take it from them for it shall be engraven upon their heart. I speak unto them which shall accept it as their own and it shall be unto them a shield and buckler in the time of stress. I say they shall work with this until it becomes their own. And it shall not be misused or spoken idly for it is the sayings of the unwise which are the parts of the idolators and the hypocrites. I say ye shall engrave this part upon thy heart. Make it thy own and great shall be thy reward. So be it and Selah.

Be ye blest O my child and hear that which I say unto thee. I would deliver thee out this day, and yet ye would not be as one prepared to enter into my place of abode. All things are done according to the law. So be it and Selah.

Ye shall now take these words which I shall give unto thee as thy own and engrave them forever upon thy eternal heart.

Beloved spirit God - Father Mother - which has caused me to be. Send forth thy radiant love thy consciousness through me that I might glorify thee in the earth that all men might be drawn into thy light and receive of thy love and life without limitation.

I ask of thee that all men might know that which is their live divine inheritance willed unto them of God the Father - thou art the Father Mother God and unto thee all the praise and the glory forever and forever. Amen. So be it.

I come unto thee that all mankind might be blest - such is my love for them and such is thy will that all men everywhere be brought out of bondage.

O Father Mother God I do give thanks this day for thy being that thou hast seen fit to give unto me being that I might go forth as thou would have me - that I might walk among them as man as woman - I am glad.

Give unto me this day the power and energy to walk as thou would have me - no other gods shall I have save thee. Blest am I. Blest O my soul. Praise him which has sent me forth. Amen and Selah.

Recorded by Sister Thedra of the Emerald Cross

Sorica-- "The water from the wine--salt from the sand..."

Sorica speaking unto thee. Be ye as one blest of me and by me for it is now come when I shall speak unto thee of things which are new and strange unto thee and ye shall be given comprehension for these things are given at this time for the few which shall be given comprehension. I say that the few which are now prepared shall comprehend. And them which prepared shall be given comprehension and they shall receive as they are prepared. For in no wise shall they be given that which is unwise or unjust. I say they which have ears to hear shall hear -- and they which have eyes shall see -- for it is near the time for the gathering in when the water shall be divided from the wine and the salt shall be divided from the sand. And the sheep shall be divided from the goats and the servant shall sup with the master and the lion shall lie down with the lamb.

And the goat shall suckle the child and the wattling shall nest on the water. I say ye shall be as one prepared for strange new things and ye shall be up and about thy Father's business for ye shall be as ones true unto thyself for there are none so sad as the ones which betray themselves. So be it that when the drought is ended it shall be turbulent waters from the north and sleet shall cover the fields in the dry and parched lands. I say ye have seen the last day before the end cometh.

I say ye liveth in the last days of the old cycle. Ye likewise liveth in the beginning of the new. And the old shall pass away and all things shall become new. And for this be ye glad. Sing ye praise that this day is come and that the old is past. There shall be a glad new day and peace shall reign and ye shall be as ones which have heralded in this new order. Ye have gone through the fire and come through victorious. And ye shall be glad for thy victory!

Ye which hear these my words shall remember them well for ye shall be caused to remember them --- for ye shall be as ones which shall have thy memory restored unto thee. For this give thanks. Praise the name of Solen Solen Aum Solen. Praise unto the Father Mother God. Praise Him all ye of the earth.

Amen and Selah. I am thy sibor and thy brother, Sorica.

Recorded by Sister Thedra of the Emerald Cross

Sorica-- "he shall have the seal of Solomon"

Sorica speaking. Be ye blest of me and by me -- for this do I come. I speak upon a subject which is new unto thee. I say that which ye have not heard - and which ye have not seen. I say unto thee, that there are great and powerful forces which now surround the place wherein ye are -- and these forces are not of earth nor are they created by man. These forces are for thy protection and for thy welfare.

I say that the ones which are not prepared for the greater work shall be unable to stand before this power -- for great indeed it is! I say that it is indeed great! And they which are prepared for to receive of such strength and power shall be as ones which are prepared to enter into the temple wherein is the altar of white alabaster. I say that the temple wherein stands the white altar shall be the place of thy great initiation and the place of thy unveiling. So be it that they which do go out from this temple shall find them which are ready and they shall bring them in. I say they which have prepared themself shall be brought in. And great shall be their joy. I say unto them it is worth all thy effort. So be it and Selah.

I speak unto them which are yet in darkness -- and they which are afraid and which give unto themself credit for being wise.

Ye shall be as ones which have been given much and ye shall be likened unto one which has gone unto the ocean with a cloth sack which is absorbs little moisture and carries none with thee. For ye have been given the laws governing thy preparation and ye have as yet not heeded that which has been said. Ye have wandered to and fro. Ye have waved to and fro as the willow in the wind. I say ye have waxed hot and cold. Ye have gone out - and ye have come in - and ye have said many things which ye know not. Ye have been as the unknowing ones.

Now let this be recorded for them which are fortuned to read. There shall be one which shall make his appearance in the place wherein ye are and he shall be as one which has his hand in the hand of the Lord Sananda, Son of God, and he shall walk as man and he shall speak as man, yet he shall be of a different species. He shall be as one sent of God the Father for this part. He shall have upon his head the Crown of the Sun and upon his brow the Seal of Solomon and he shall be as none other.

And he shall walk among them and seek out them which are prepared to be brought out from among them. And he shall bring them into the place wherein I am and he shall bless them as he has been blest. Such shall be his mission. And it shall be accomplished with honor and dignity. So be it the Father's will. Amen and Selah.

I am Sorica, Son of God the Father.

Recorded by Sister Thedra of the Emerald Cross

Berean-- The Coming of the KING

Berean speaking unto thee from out the center of creation. I come unto thee that they might have these my words. Blest are they which do receive them -- they which shall make them their own - for they shall be as one prepared for the part which has been held in trust for them.

I say unto them: that within this day one shall take embodiment thru woman and he shall not be of earth -- he shall not be of the seed of man -- he shall be of the "light" -- he shall be conceived of "light" -- he shall be the Father made manifest thru woman.

He shall be the Father incarnate upon earth -- for the first time has this been, which is to be. And the one which is to come shall be called "Born" and he shall be as none other -- for he shall be as the King of Glory -- he shall bring with him a host from the realms of light and he shall bring with him The Lord of Hosts -- the Wearer of the Golden Helmet shall he bring. He shall bring with him a legion of workers from the temple of Osiris, and from the temple of Born. And I say ye which are prepared shall walk with them and talk with them. I say greater things than these shall ye do -- for mighty is the power of the Lord thy God.

I say great is the preparation this day within all the secret places of earth for his coming. And great is the joy that this day is come. So be it and Selah.

I am come that the way may be made clear. So be it and Selah. I shall speak unto thee from out the place wherein I am and ye shall hear me. So be it shall profit thee. Amen. So be it.

I am Berean, Son of God.

Recorded by Sister Thedra of the Emerald Cross

Berean-- "No hiding place"

Berean speaking unto thee. Be ye as my hand made manifest unto them which shall be fortuned to read these words. I say unto thee ye shall say unto them as I would say - that the day of the Lord is at hand. And I say unto them they shall arise and put off the old and take up the banner of the Lord and they shall carry it high and they shall be as ones which go out before him.

I say he shall be as one which comes when they have been prepared to receive him -- he shall come unto the ones prepared to receive him and he shall know them - for he is not misled. He knows where to find thee and he looks not in vain - for he knows wherein ye are. I say there is no hiding place -- and ye shall be as ones true unto thyself and prepare thyself for great shall be thy joy.

I say ye which are not prepared shall be as ones which have betrayed thyself - and they are the saddest of the lot. Be ye as ones which have upon thy shoulders the responsibility of thy own salvation. Such is the law.

Hear ye these words for I do proclaim unto thee a truth. As I say unto thee that in the days just ahead he, the Lord, shall walk with them which are prepared to receive him and he shall give unto them instruction such as shall prepare them for the greater part -- and they shall be brought into one of the secret places which have been held in trust for this day and for this purpose. I say that there are schools which are established and held ready to receive the ones which have and do qualify to enter therein and it is the better part of wisdom to prepare thyself to enter therein. For in the time which is now at hand many shall be gathered together for the purpose of learning the laws which have hitherto been unrevealed.

I say that among these is the transmutation of the dense form - the title pore - the physical body - into the substance of light. And when this is accomplished ye shall be as one free from all bondage - forever free. I say this is freedom--eternal freedom! So be it and Selah. Praise ye the name of God the Father forever for his mercy and his power shall be known throughout all the cosmos. Praise ye all the peoples of the earth. Praise him forever.

I shall speak with thee again and again.

I am Berean,

Recorded by Sister Thedra of the Emerald Cross

BEREAN The Badge of Recognition

Berean speaking. Beloved of my being ye shall now say unto them in my name and as I would say: That one shall walk in their midst and that one shall have upon his head the Crown of the Sun and upon his forehead the Seal of Solomon.

And he shall move silently among them and he shall know them; by their works shall he know them.

He shall place upon them a mark which shall be unto them their badge of recognition one unto the other.

He shall give unto them a number and a color and he shall speak the word which shall become manifest and ye shall step from thy old body into thy holy Christ body which shall not bind thee.

I say one shall pass among them and he shall seek out them which are prepared to receive him and of him.

He shall give unto them the water of life and he shall speak "The Word" which shall become manifest. And they which are so prepared shall step forth from their dense form of chemical substance into the body of light substance as ones purified and as ones glorified of the Father. So be it and Selah.

I say that when they prepare themself for this the greater part their reward shall be their Godhood. So be it as the Father has willed it. Amen and Selah.

Be ye as one prepared to receive the greater part. So be it, it shall profit thee.

I am come that ye may be, brought out of bondage forever and forever.

Be ye blest this day -- remember this day and keep it holy. And be ye as one which has the mind to comprehend that which I have said unto thee.

Be ye blest of me and by me for I shall be within the secret place to welcome thee. So be it and Selah.

I am glad this day is come. I am thy brother and thy sibor, Berean.

Recorded by Sister Thedra of the Emerald Cross

BOREA One of the El O Heim

Borea speaking. Beloved of my being, be ye blest of me and by me. I come that ye may be blest. So be it I come unto thee from out the heart of creation. I come as one which creates like unto the Father. I come as one of the El-o-heim. I come as one present with thee always. I come that they might know me. I come that they all may be blest.

I come as one prepared for this day -- and I say unto thee that they might have these words which are for the good of all mankind. In this day shall the doors be opened unto the kingdom of heaven and ye shall pass both ways. Ye shall go and come freely and without limitation. I say all which have prepared themself shall pass the great barrier without limitations. There shall be no limitation unto them which are true unto themself and walk according to the law set before them.

I come that ye might be strengthened in all thy weak parts and ye shall be given the strength to endure all things. I say ye shall have thy strength renewed. And thy soul shall rejoice forever that it is accomplished. I say ye shall endure unto the end. And ye shall be glad. So be it and Selah.

I come unto thee as one full of grace and love -- and I am because the Father Mother is -- and I know myself to be one with them. I have not separated myself from them and I am glad.

I come unto thee as one prepared to give unto thee a hand that ye might be lifted up. And ye shall be as one which has the mind to be lifted up. Ye shall apply thyself and ye shall glorify the Father in the earth and give unto him all the praise and the glory. And walk in the way set before thee and ye shall ask of The Father for light and he shall not turn thee away.

Such is my part -- to bring unto thee love and to minister unto thee in the hours of thy sleep. And I say unto thee there are ones among thee which walk with me and talk with me while their physical body does sleep. Yet they are alert -- and they are willing to learn and they ask for light and they are as ones which come in great love and humility and return rejoicing. Be ye blest this day and I shall speak with thee again and again. I am thy sister Borea - born of God the Father. Amen so be it.

Recorded by Sister Thedra of the Emerald Cross

Through the hand of Sorea Sorea

Be thee ever mindful of thy heritage and walk in the Light thereof. My hand will ever steady thee when ye reach unto me.

But first ye must free thyself of all thy doubts and fears which are as leg irons unto thee, keeping thee in bondage. Ye are as free as ye think ye are.

No man can change ye. Ye are thy own masters and makers of thy own fate. No one is to be made to change his thinking or his actions. Thou shall not expect thy Sibors to do that which is for thee alone to do.

I walk with thee if thou desire me.

I give unto thee strength.

I give unto thee truth.

I give unto thee hope.

I give unto thee courage.

I give unto thee wisdom.

I give unto thee love.

I give unto thee all that ye ask that is for the highest good-- and the good of all. Ye have but to ask and I hear thee.

Thy Light shall shine forth to bless all who have the will to see - and many shall be drawn to thy light and ye shall lead them home.

And ye shall heal the sick and comfort the mournful.

Ye shall be as outposts of the Master's power - and ye shall do all he asks of thee and thy blessings shall flow as the pure waters of a mighty spring giving life unto thee - and all who will may receive of thee this pure water of life - and thy blessing will multiply and bear the fruit of life everlasting for all who partake.

All who will may come and I will make them welcome.

Rejoice and be exceedingly glad for this opportunity for thy cup shall runneth over.

I am thy sibor and thy older brother Sananda.

Recorded by Sorea Sorea.

"Be Steadfast in Thy Righteousness"

Borea speaking - Be ye as one blest of me and by me. I am come unto thee that they may come to know me. I come unto thee that all mankind might be blest of me through thee.

I come that they might be lifted up. I come that they might know as I know. I come that there might be no more sorrow and suffering upon the little red star --

I come that she might be celebrated, that she might come into the fullness of her heritage. Such is my part to give unto them that which has been kept for them for this day. And I say unto thee the few which are prepared to receive me shall be glad this day is come.

I come unto thee from out the center of Creation -- I come as one which has been given the power and the authority to create like unto the Father - in His Image do I create --

I am come unto thee through the Council of the great white brotherhood -- It is with their consent which has watched thy progress that I come. I say unto them which do read these my words - that it is given unto many to be called and few are chosen.

So be it a great COMMAND - "Be ye about thy Father's business, for the day of The Lord is now come."

Be ye about thy own preparation and turn neither to the left nor to the right. Be ye steadfast in thy righteousness. Be ye as one which has a crown upon thy head and walk which way it tilts not. Be ye as one which can keep thy silence - and know when it is wise to break it.

I say unto thee which do read these words: It is now come when thy words shall manifest before thee - ye shall take thought of the power of the spoken word - and ye shall take heed of that which goes out of thy mouth. So be it that thy words shall return unto thee to bless or to displease thee. I say they shall return unto thee as the fowls of the air unto their roosting place.

Bless them which misuse thee. Give unto them thy love - and be no part of their foolishness. Be ye a lamp unto their feet. Be no part of frivolity - and the part which is fortuned unto the foolish.

Be ye as one which can carry thy own burden as one graceful and without hatred. Be ye glad for thy strength and bless thy benefactors which have directed such energy (as ye use) unto thee.

Be ye mindful of all thy blessings. Give unto the Father all the Glory and all the credit. So be it ye shall give unto thyself credit for being a Son of God the Father. Bless thyself - and be ye blest of me this day. I am thy sister Borea.

New Part New Place

Berea speaking: Be ye blest of me this day - and ye shall hear my words - for I shall speak unto thee--for the first time shall my words be audible unto thee, and ye shall be as one prepared to hear them. For it is now come when ye shall be given another part which shall be new unto thee, and ye shall be as none other - nor shall thy part be like unto any other's part. I say ye shall be given a part separate from all others - for no two shall be given the same parts. Yet all parts are one--of the great whole. I say it is one part -- given in many "parts" - in many ways.

For there are many people within the world of man and it is a necessary to reach each one on his own level - for there are various levels of consciousness - and each is as a separate one - and yet each is as one - there is no separation - only in appearance. I say they appear to be many - yet there is no separation.

This is Truth - and truth is that which is eternal and which shall always remain as state of Being God -- that which changes not. And yet that which changes not takes unto itself various sounds - color-tone and certain vibrations - radiations and form. I say that which is changeless does change the substance of the etheric matter which also is God - and that which has gone out from Him that he might glorify Himself.

That which is changeless-let us call it life - is the first cause of form and color - motion and sound. That which has color and sound is life and it vibrates at a rate which is of another rate or vibration which is unlike any other form - or sound - thus the various parts of creation made manifest upon worlds without end.

Be ye as one prepared for thy new part and I shall direct thee into a place wherein there shall be great activity wherein there shall be great love and harmony.

I say peace shall abide with thee and ye shall be as one blest forever, so be it and Selah.

I am thy older sister and I come as such that ye may be sustained in thy hours of trial -- such is my word unto thee, so be it and Selah.

I am Berea. (Berea is the compliment of Sanat Kumara -- this is the name they give to me -- she is also known by others. Thedra.)

"The Chosen"

Berea speaking -- Be ye as my hand made manifest unto them - and say unto them as I would say that there are many called - and few are chosen.

Yet the few which are chosen shall be as ones prepared through their own effort. And they shall be as the seed of the new earth and they shall endure unto the end.

Such is my word unto the chosen. The ones chosen shall be chosen for their fitness to serve within the holy places -- wherein they shall find great work prepared for them -- wherein they shall find ones which have gone before them waiting to train - to teach - to illumine them -- to "sibor" them in the new part which shall be given unto them. I say that they which are chosen shall be brought into the holy temple wherein they shall be sibored in the laws which have hitherto not been revealed -- such as pertaining unto their work or unto their "part."

I say that each shall have a part separate and unlike another, for it is not given unto us to go into complicated work and do the work of another. And each is fully responsible for his own part and none trespasses upon that of the other. I say unto thee we do not complicate the law -- man does that.

We simplify -- we go not into the dark for light -- we go to the light that darkness might forever be banished from the earth. So be it and Selah.

I am come that ye might have light for I am one with the Father Mother God. And I know myself to be. I am one with thee. I know thee as I know myself for I am conscious of my Source of Being.

Be ye blest of me and by me this day. I am come that ye may be blest. Amen so be it and Selah.

Berea

BEREA - TWIN RAY

Berea speaking unto thee - that they might have these my words. I say unto them which are yet bound in the world of men that there are none so foolish as the ones which think themself wise and none so sad as he who betrays himself or his trust.

It is indeed a great truth and when this lesson is learned ye are ready to begin thy work - thy preparation for the greater part. So be it the first lesson ye shall learn. I say when the initiate begins his work he learns this lesson: He learns that there are greater things in the universe than he has dreamed of. So be it he walks in the way set before him with the hand in his sibors' -- his head high, his eye single and his mind set upon his goal. He is not divided. He meditates upon the laws set before him. He walks as though he had a crown upon his head and he walks not in the footsteps of the transgressor. He gives unto his benefactors credit for knowing that which they say and do. He gives unto the Father all the credit for his being -- yet he gives unto his benefactors credit for his well-being.

He has won the first battle when he reaches the first rung of the ladder and I say there are many. He which is opinionated shall be among the wanton and among the unlearned, for thy opinions shall be as tacks in thy shoes.

It is said, "Come as a little child and I shall give unto thee water which ye know not of." So be it and Selah. I say they shall come as a little child and they shall bring with them no thing! Nothing. They shall find all their inheritance intact which has been kept for them. So be it and Selah.

I say when it is come that they have finished their mission within the earth and have returned victorious. They shall be united with and unto their ray which has waited and they shall be in twain no more -- forever shall they be united and therein is another story.

I shall speak with thee at length upon that. So be it, it shall wait. I am thy sister and thy Sibor Berea.

THE KING OF GLORY COMETH

Berea speaking: Be ye blest of me this day and ye shall be unto them my hand made manifest unto them. Be ye as my mouth and my voice and say unto them as I would say: that it is now come when one shall walk among them and he shall be of the Father send and he shall be the King of Glory! I say he shall be the King of Glory -- so be it he shall be the Father incarnate in flesh - he shall be the one for which ye have waited. I say he shall come as one born of woman, and he shall be as others in appearance, yet he shall be as none other. So be it and Selah.

I say he shall be as none other for he has not been born of woman. He has not taken upon himself hu-man form. He is of virgin spirit. He has not taken unto himself the form of flesh. He has not been in the realm of darkness as one bound. He shall come as one of flesh yet it shall not bind him nor shall it limit him. He shall be the form of man and he shall be of the mind of the Father for his memory shall not be blanked from him. He shall retain his memory. So be it the Father's will.

I say unto them which have the mind to comprehend that the day of fulfillment is now come when all thy prophecies shall be fulfilled and ye shall live to see the Son of Man walk among thee, for he shall be there upon thy planet earth to receive the King of Glory. He is The Wayshower and he is the giver of the law. He is the director of this new dispensation and he brings unto the new law and the herald of the coming. He speaks unto thee of the coming and ye hear not that which he says. Be ye as one which has a will to hear and to comprehend that which ye hear. I say ye shall be given great revelation when ye are so minded. So be it and Selah.

Hail the King! Hail the King! The King of Glory cometh. I say he cometh. And the day is not afar off. Be ye as ones prepared that ye might be caught up with him. Praise him all ye nations of the earth. Praise him all ye people of the earth. Give unto him all the praise and the glory forever and forever. Amen and Selah.

Be ye as ones prepared for this day when the gates of heaven swing wide and they shall go in and out as ones of earth and heaven -- the earth shall receive the hosts of the realms of light, and heaven shall receive the children of Earth. And the seers shall see and we thy guardians shall be glad this day is come.

For long we have waited when we might be unto thee guests -- when we might come unto thee as such and be received with love and in peace and with understanding.

Praise the Father for his mercy and his grace -- it shall abide with in the holy places wherein there is only Love and Peace.

Blest are they which find such peace. Blest are they for they shall go out no more. So be it and Selah.

I am with thee unto the end. I am thy sibor and thy older sister, Berea.

THE ETERNAL MOTHER

Sarah speaking: Beloved of my bosom -- beloved of my being -- of my heart -- I have given myself that ye might be.

I have given unto thee expression.

I have given unto thee the will to be as one prepared to return unto the place of thy going out.

I have waited thy return. I have longed for thy return. I have held thee fast in the hours of thy unknowing. I have given unto thee words which have astonished thee when they proceeded from thy lips. I have manifested before thee in many forms. I have given unto thee strength to overcome thy weakness.

I have put within thy hand mine. I have led thee through the hours of despair. I have gone into the depths with thee. I have climbed the summits with thee. I have gone into the dragon's den that ye might be blest of me. I have gone into the temples of many a planet with thee that ye might have light.

I have been unto thee thy guiding light.

I have brought thee into this place wherein ye shall be as my hand made manifest unto them. And ye shall say unto them as I would say that "there shall be the two -- one shall be taken and the other left -- many are called and few are chosen." So be it and Selah. I say they which are chosen are chosen for their fitness and for their ability to learn. I say they which are of a mind to learn shall be as ones prepared for the greater part.

Yet it is necessary to put aside the old and put on the new. I say that the old shall be put off and the new shall be put on. Too I say as ye are prepared so shall ye receive -- such is the law. I say that when ye come unto the altar which the Father has caused to be set up as a little child and asked for light, unopinionated and with contrite heart ye shall be answered.

Ye shall ask of him thy freedom from bondage and he shall hear thee and answer thee. So be it and Selah.

I say that none shall tell him what he shall do - and he which says that which the Father shall do is the greatest of fools.

I say they are as ones bound in darkness. They know not. I say they are the unknowing ones.

Be ye as one which can come unto this altar clean of hands and of heart and ye shall be lifted up.

So be it I come that they may all be brought out of bondage. So be it and Selah.

I am thy Mother eternal.

Recorded by Thedra

BEREA-SANAT KUMARA... SPOUSE ETERNAL

Berea speaking: Be ye as my hand made manifest -- and say unto them as I would say -- that I am one with Sanat Kumara as his right hand, as his one and only spouse eternal. I am eternally wed with him. I am not separated from him, and I am not to be separated from him.

I am known by other names -- yet I speak unto thee as Berea. For it is given unto me to be Berea, and that is another story. I come that they may know me and I am now prepared to speak at length on many subjects which shall enlighten them, and they shall profit thereby.

I say I shall speak on many subjects at length in the time which is near and it shall profit them. So be it and Selah. I say ye shall be as my hand made manifest unto them, for ye have been unto me as one prepared for this part and I find thee acceptable. So be it I am glad. They shall be as ones blest by me and of me.

Now ye shall say unto them that there shall be a gathering in. And they shall be brought together as the brides and bridegrooms. They shall return unto their places of abode -- unto the place from which they went out. I say they which are brought together for the fulfillment of the covenant shall be brought in as the brides and bridegrooms. So be it there shall be many -- and the joy shall abound within the place wherein I am for I say they shall be brought in as a part of the host -- for they shall be part of the great army which shall go out with the King of Glory.

He shall be as one which is to be born of woman - and the brides and bridegrooms shall make up the great part of the host which shall attend him, so be it and Selah. I shall speak of this again, so be it and Selah. I am Berea, sister of the Emerald Cross.

BEREA - SANAT KUMARA

Brides-Bridegrooms

Berea speaking: Beloved of our being -- be ye blest this day. I come as Berea, for I speak for the two which is one -- never to be separated -- and I say unto thee that in the time which is now at hand that many shall be united through the first law -- the law of "completeness" -- the law of "oneness" -- the law of "perfection."

I say unto thee that they might have these my words -- that it is now come when many shall be brought in and united as the brides and bridegrooms of God the Father. I say that it is now come when these things shall be accomplished which have been referred to in thy holy writ. They have not been understood by the ones which have placed their own interpretation upon them.

I say it is now come when these things shall be common knowledge and ye shall be given the comprehension which is of the initiate. I say that ye shall now come to know the meaning of these things which have been so maltreated by the uninitiated.

I say I shall speak with thee on many subjects and this one is dear unto my heart. For I see so much unreal love and sorrow and suffering because of thy unknowing. I say it is now come when great light shall be shed upon the hitherto mysteries of life upon the planet earth. I say that great light shall be shed upon the "hitherto" mysteries and there shall be no more mystery concerning these things.

I say that I see and know that which causes all thy sorrows and suffering. And they are as nothing when the cause is understood - and when ye do work with the law which is given unto thee from the beginning.

So be it that I speak unto all mankind at this time that there might be peace among thee.

I say from the beginning of thy going out from the Father-Mother God (dual in principal) that ye were made in their likeness and in their "Image." They "imaged" thee and they sent thee forth as one: as one made perfect and complete. I say ye were as one - completed in perfect oneness as man - as <u>man</u>ifestation of God the parent - Mother.

I say when ye divided thyself ye did it of thy own free will. Ye gave unto the Father thy vow that ye should return unto him and take up thy sword and thy shield.

Let this not be misunderstood by the ones which think themself wise. I say thy sword and thy shield is the armor of God the Father - the power, the truth, the Law, the understanding of the law, the fulfilling of the law, and the will to do. I say that the fulfilling of the law is the will of God.

And when ye have the will to follow within the law set before thee from this day forth ye shall be within the protection and under the guidance of the Great "White Star" -- the Order of Melchezedec and the Order of the Emerald Cross.

I say unto thee these are not orders of man nor of earth. These orders are of divine origin and are composed of the federations of many systems and galaxies throughout the cosmos.

I come unto thee through the Order of the Emerald Cross. I speak unto thee as Berea and Sanat Kumara -- I am his female counterpart. I am one eternally wed with him and I am glad. So be it and Selah. Berea.

Ye Are Not Alone---the POWER of the Word

Sarah speaking -- Beloved of my being be ye blest of me and by me for I come unto thee that ye may be blest. I say unto thee it is now come when great shall be thy revelations. I say that great things shall be revealed unto thee and it is so. So be it.

I come that they may have light - that all men might have light. So be it and Selah. I speak unto thee these words that they may have them and that they might learn of me, and that they might be brought out of bondage. Such is my love for them.

I say that they are not alone in their little world which they create for themself. I say they are not alone upon the tiny "red star" - "Terra." They are not alone in their hiding places for I say unto them there is no hiding place! for they are not alone. I say there are no secrets: Only their unknowing which is the result of having their memory blanked from them.

I say when their memory was blanked from them they went into darkness -- and they lost the power of the "word" which was God and which is God. I say they are not enlightened in their knowing --

they are as ones groping in darkness. They have the memory stored in the secret closet wherein they file all their deeds - all their opinions - all their guilt - all their sorrows - and these they lock safely within their own secret place wherein they go in the hours of their sleep, and recount their experiences one by one as their rosaries. And they cherish the memory of that which has given unto them pleasure of the animal senses - animal nature and they are as ones bound unto these things which have given unto them pleasure and sorrow - until they free themself from the animal nature - the senses - which are of the animal kingdom.

Such is the law. I say ye are as one bound by these senses until ye have purified thy own self of every vestige of the animal senses- the anger passions of the animal and the grossness which belong unto the animal kingdom.

I say ye shall go into thy secret place and bring out all that which ye have buried therein and examine it, remember it - for that which it is. Forgive thyself for thy foolishness and thy unknowing - unlock thy "leg irons" and turn from them and walk away from them as one unbound as a free man. I say unto thee it is that simple. I say ye alone can unlock thy leg irons.

We of the golden helmeted ones can but show the way. We can but point out the pitfalls and lead thee up and direct thee. Yet I say ye shall walk in the way set before thee. I say ye shall be as ones which have a mind to learn and the will. And one shall be sent unto thee which shall bring thee out of the place wherein ye are and ye shall find a place prepared for thee wherein ye may dwell throughout all eternity - in freedom and in light and love which is, which was, and ever shall be - worlds without end. So be it and Selah. I am thy Mother eternal. Sarah.

Recorded by Sister Thedra

STEPHANI

"The Initiates Walk Among Us"

Beloved of my being: BE YE as one blest of me and by me. I come unto thee that they might have this my word.

I say unto them which are yet within the world of men -- that when it is come that they are delivered up they shall be as ones wise -- they shall be as ones celebrated, and they shall be as ones which have received their sonship of God the Father. I say many of the Sons of God walk among thee free from any and all limitation. Yet they appear even as ye -- for they move in silence -- they flaunt not their wisdom nor their learning before man. They speak wisely and prudently. They know when to speak -- and poised are they. And they are at peace for they know themself for that which they are.

They have no false gods - neither do they bow down unto any man, for they fear no man - no thing -- they carry within their hand the "rod of power" -- they carry no weapons -- only the sword of truth -- the two-edged sword, and they are as ones prepared for any occasion.

I speak unto thee from out the monitor ship the XTX and upon which are many which are being prepared to go forth as ones which shall walk among thee as emissaries, and they shall find thee -- that is, they shall find the ones which are prepared and which are found trustworthy and worth the effort. I say the ones which have a will to serve unto the end -- which are prepared to endure all things according to the law. And the ones which are obedient unto the law shall be found and given assistance and they shall be as ones which are the servants, and they shall serve in the great and divine plan. I say that they shall serve the plan which is designed to deliver all mankind from bondage forever.

Now I speak unto them which have a will to serve. Be ye alert and give unto the Father credit for thy being and unto thy benefactors credit for thy well-being, and they shall give unto thee a hand. So be it and Selah. I am Stephani.

"There shall be great suffering..."

Sanat Kumara speaking: Be ye blest of my presence and of my being. I come that ye may be blest. I give unto thee my love and of my time that ye might be blest. I speak unto thee this day as one which has gone before thee that ye might find thy way. I speak unto thee that ye might find thy way -- yet he shall be as ones responsible for thy own preparation and ye shall walk in the way set before thee.

I say the law is clearly stated and ye shall apply thyself -- in all thy ways ye shall remember that which has been given unto thee. I say ye shall profit thereby. And give no thing unto them which they can use against thee. I say ye shall keep for thyself that which is given unto thee: and that which is given unto thee for them give unto them. And they shall receive it in the name of the Father, Son and Holy Ghost, amen and Selah. I say ye shall say unto them as I would say that they shall bear witness of these my words and they shall remember them for it is given unto me to see and to know that which is - that which shall be and that which has been.

It is now come when there shall be mighty winds and there shall be great suffering and much sorrow. And there shall be many homeless and fraught with fear and disease.

And ye shall be as ones which have upon thy shoulders great responsibility, for ye shall be as ones prepared to bring comfort and peace wherein there is no comfort and no peace. I say ye shall prepare thyself for that which shall be given unto thee to do. So be it and Selah. I say ye shall prepare thyself for thy part and when this is done we thy sibors shall do our part.

I say unto them which are yet in the sleepers realm that they shall alert themself and they shall awaken and be up and about the Father's business. I say ye have slept overtime. Too I say that great is the work which is accomplished while ye have slept. While ye have slept many have walked thy highways and thy byways which have within their hand the power to deliver thee up. Yet ye have not recognized them nor have ye asked that ye know them. Ye are bound by thy own opinions and by thy dogmas. I say ye are bound by thy own opinions and by thy own dogmas. Ye shall be as ones free from all opinions, from all dogma Ye shall stand as one free from all bondage forever.

I say ye shall ask of God the Father for LIGHT and for thy freedom. Such shall profit thee. So be it and Selah.

I am thy older brother Sanat Kumara.

Thou shall --Thou shall not - Berea

Berea speaking: Beloved of my being- be ye blest this day of me and by me. I come that ye may be blest- so be it and Selah.

Be ye as one prepared for the greater part--

I say ye shall be as one on whose shoulders rests great responsibility- for ye shall go out from the place wherein ye are as one prepared----

I say: Ye shall go out from the place wherein ye are as one prepared- so be it and Selah---

Be ye as my hand made manifest unto them which shall read these words- and they shall bear witness of that which I say--they shall remember these words and they shall not desecrate them.

Be as ones which have a mind to comprehend these things which I say unto thee and comprehension shall be given unto thee--

Ye shall NOW be as ones willing to follow in the footsteps of the WAYSHOWER--

Ye shall walk in the way he sets before thee--

Ye shall prepare thyself--

Ye shall do that which he commands of thee--

Ye shall be as ones brought out from among them--- (the world)

Ye shall be no part of their foolishness---

Ye shall not join in the foolish parts which they fortune unto themself--

Ye shall be as a thing apart--

Ye shall dare to be different from "them"--

Ye shall stand as the <u>rock</u> - and ye shall be unmoved---

Ye shall hold steadfast unto RIGHTEOUSNESS---

Ye shall plant thy feet on the solid rock- hold thy head high and KNOW I AM GOD-- THE SON of GOD I AM- and nothing shall touch thee- so be it and Selah.

I come unto thee that this may be given unto them and they shall have it at the earliest time possible- so be it and Selah. I am with thee unto the end. I am thy older sister and sibor, Berea.

Recorded by Sister Thedra of the Emerald Cross

BEREA -- "Be ye single of eye..."

Berea speaking: Beloved of my being, be ye as my hand unto them and say unto them as I would say that there are many among them which are prepared to give unto them the water of life. And they walk among thee. Ye shall prepare thyself and give unto thy preparation the proper attention and ye shall be glad. For it is now come when great shall be thy trials and temptations. Ye shall be alert

-- and ye shall be as ones which have thy eye single and thy heart fixed upon thy goal.

I say ye shall not divide thyself. Ye shall be as <u>one</u>. Ye shall be as "one undivided." It is said that ye have divided thy time, spent thy energy in frivolity. And ye have gone the long way to serve the forces of darkness. Ye have been unto thyself traitor. Ye are as yet bound by the forces of darkness. I say the dragon is not of a mind to release thee. He shall fight unto the last to hold thee fast. So be it ye shall will thy freedom -- alert thyself and he shall not pursue thee.

I say he shall not hold thee against thy will. Be ye blest of them which are sent that ye might have thy freedom. So be it that it shall profit thee to reach out and accept that which we offer unto thee in the name of the most high living God. So be it and Selah.

I say unto thee we are of the Father sent and we give unto thee as he gives unto us for thee. So be it and Selah.

I come that ye may have the greater part. Such is my love for thee. I join my beloved Sanat Kumara in this endeavor that the fullness of the plan might be realized and that ye might be part of it. I say that the ones which do awaken and alert themself shall sit in council with us as part of the great and divine plan. So be it and Selah.

I say that they which are the sleepers shall sleep on. So be it and Selah. I speak unto thee from out the fullness of my heart and I know whereof I speak. So be it and Selah. I am with thee and ye have but to accept me - my love. My hand and I shall make known unto thee many wonderful things. So be it and Selah.

I am thy older sister - thy sibor, Berea.

Recorded by Sister Thedra of the Emerald Cross

BEREA -- The Signs - the end of the age...

Berea speaking: Be ye blest of my being - and say unto them as I would say - that it is now come when they shall be as ones prepared. For when they shall see the great and glorious signs which shall be manifest from the realms of light --

And when they shall see the great darkness descend upon the earth --

And when they shall see prophecy fulfilled they shall see and know that the end of the age is come.

I say they shall see the handwriting upon the wall -- and they shall read while they run--

I say these are great signs -- and ye shall be as ones which have the mind to read - and to know the meaning thereof --

Say I unto thee - be ye of a mind to learn and great things shall be revealed unto thee. I say the signs of the times are written within the sky - within the stones - they are marked -- and the waters give up their secrets.

I say that the earth shall give up her secrets - she shall be as an open book - she shall be relieved of all her spoils - of her burden-- for she has held her secrets jealously -- and she shall be glad for her freedom. So be it she shall be freed from her bondage - forever free - for she shall pass out of her present port into clear waters wherein she shall rest -- wherein she shall have peace and rest --

Wherein she shall be prepared to receive the Sons of God which shall inherit the NEW EARTH.

I say they shall inherit the NEW EARTH - so be it and Selah. I say the earth shall be cleansed and renewed - so be it her inheritance -- so be it and Selah.

I speak unto them which are as ones yet in darkness--and I say- ye shall come to know that which is fortuned unto thee -- ye shall awaken and ye shall be as ones wise to alert thyself. For it is now come when the earth shall no longer give unto the IDOLATORS and unto the sleepers comfort -- she shall cast them off her back so be it ye shall be put into a place which has been prepared for thee--

I say - be ye as ones alert! And HEAR me! And remember these my words. And mark them well -- for they shall stand thee in good stead.

Be ye as ones which have a will to hear --

I am come that ye may be prepared for the greater part - which is thy own Godhood - so be it and Selah.

I am Berea.

Recorded by Sister Thedra of the Emerald Cross

BERIA -- "I see them..."

Berea speaking: Beloved of my being - be ye as my hand made manifest unto them -- and say unto them as I would say -- that there are ones which walk among them which are prepared to give unto them the waters of life.

I say that there is one which is come which has within his hand the power to give unto thee the crystal goblet. And ye have but to purify thyself and he shall find thee and he shall seek thee out when the hour strikes -- and ye shall be glad for thy effort. I say ye shall be glad for thy effort. Such is my word unto thee.

Be ye blest this day - and give unto them this my word and ye shall be as my hand and as my voice -- for I say unto them it is now come when many shall walk among us as ones qualified to lift them up. And they shall be alert and walk with their head high and they shall be as ones which have upon their head a crown and they shall walk which way it tilts not. So be it, it shall be becoming unto them.

I say they shall walk in the way set before them - they shall turn not to the left nor to the right --

I say they shall be as ones on whose shoulders rests the responsibility of their own salvation.

I speak unto them out of the fullness of time. I see and know. I see them as ones filled with longing - with care - with fear. I see them running to and fro - I see them going and coming. I see them as ones bowed down with grief and despair. I see them as ones bound hand and foot - knowing not by what they are bound.

I see them weary of the load which they have fortuned unto themself. I see them as ones looking for a magical formula which shall be unto them a poultice -- I see them filled with hatred - filled with shame. I see them which give unto thee the bitter cup --

I see them which withhold their hearts and their service --

I see them which are as the babblers and their tongues are as the asps --

I see them as ones unbridled --

They run riot --

Their emotions know no bounds --

They are as the ones untrained - unlearned --

They are as ones yet in darkness --

They are as ones undisciplined --

They are as children -- little children -- unlearned in the ways of the initiate.

I say they have not as yet begun their work - and they are as ones which think themself wise - so be it and Selah. I speak unto them frankly and fearlessly. I say that which is given unto me to say - and no man shall set his hand unto my mouth. For I come that they may awaken and I give not my pearls without price.

I say I give not my pearls unto babes who know not their worth.

I speak of the unlearned and of the ones which "think" themself wise.

I say unto them which are within the gate that there are none so foolish as the one which thinks himself wise - and none so sad as the one which betrays himself.

I speak unto them which serve the Father day and night. I speak unto the ones which are alert and which are of a mind to walk in the way set before them - that thy reward shall be great - thy service rewarded - thy heart shall be filled with joy and thanksgiving. Ye shall remember that which is said - ye shall apply thyself wholeheartedly - ye shall hold fast unto the law.

Ye shall not weary in that which is good.

Ye shall not join them in their foolishness.

Ye shall see them for that which they are - and not for their deeds.

Ye shall not wait for their opinion and their approval - ye shall go straightway upon thy appointed course.

Ye shall ask of the Father and he shall answer thee - ye shall have no gods before thee.

Ye shall be as his foot and as his hand made manifest upon the earth. Ye shall walk with him and talk with him and ye shall know as he knows. So be it thy inheritance. I say ye the Father is not mocked. Neither is he deceived. He is not deceived. He is not mocked.

I say he which is so foolish as to try to mimic him or to give unto him the lie - is the greatest of fools - poor in spirit are they.

I say ye shall be blest of me this day. Ye have received me this day in the name of The Father, Son and Holy Ghost. So be it I shall remember thee.

I am Berea.

Recorded by Sister Thedra of the Emerald Cross

"Nothing shall be added to--" Berean

Beloved of my being--I speak with thee this day that they might know me:--

I come unto thee that they may know me--

I say unto them that there are many which walk among them as man which would give unto them the water of LIFE and I say unto them they shall be as ones prepared to receive of him--for they walk among thee--and they seek out them which are prepared and they shall be the hand of the Father--they shall put out their hand and it shall be filled--so be it the law as ye are prepared so shell ye receive.

Ye shall be about thy preparation--for none other shall be responsible for thee-- so be it and Selah---

I say unto thee that which is given unto me to say of the Father--for I speak that which He wills that I say--I speak as He would speak--

Be ye as one which has the mind to hear--and the will to do--be ye as one prepared for the NEW DAY--when all things shall be made NEW--when the OLD shall pass away--and the SONS of God shall inherit the NEW EARTH-- and the NEW HEAVENS--

Be ye as ONE responsible for thy own preparation--I say the law is clearly written - within these times - and that which has been recorded within this temple at this altar is true---

Truth! untampered with-- I say it is that which has been spoken from out the realms of light-- and by the enlightened ones.

I say NOT ONE WORD shall be misplaced-- or taken away--I say nothing shall be added to--

I say that the recorder of these scripts has been - and is - TRUE unto herself-- and I say she has OBEYED every commandment-- and too I say she shall not want--she shall be rewarded as a faithful servant--this is my word unto thee - so be it and Selah---

Now I say unto thee which I call the faithful servant: Ye shall make a copy of this and send it unto the ones referred to as Unit No. 3--and they shall bear witness of these my words---

I sign myself Berean--

Recorded by Sister Thedra of the Emerald Cross

"PEACE AND POISE"

Beloved of My being- Be ye blest of My presence and of My being- I come that you may be blest- so be it and Selah.

I speak unto thee for the good of all mankind so let it be--

Be ye as My hand made manifest unto them which are of a mind to hear that which I say unto them: --

I say unto them that when it is come that they are called to "COME OUT FROM AMONG THEM" that it is a great plan which has been given unto us thy benefactors which see and know the whole plan--

Yet I say that when we give unto thee that which ye know not ye are oft times fearful and disobedient- ye are fearful of being deceived- for the ones which would misuse thee and deceive thee use many guises and many ruses- I say they will go to the end to distract and confuse thee- so be ye as wise as the serpent and firm as the rock-

Be ye of a mind to give unto the Father thy whole heart, thy hand and thy will- and ask of HIM thy freedom--

And I say unto thee: NOTHING shall come nigh unto thee which is of darkness.

Let not thy fears consume thee. Be ye not fearful- for I say unto thee ye shall be brought out of bondage- So be it and Selah.

I come that ye may be brought out and I am glad this day is come when ye might know the plan which has been brought forth--

I say the plan is designed for this day when ye may return unto thy source without tasting of death- such is the plan.

Now I would say unto thee one word which shall stand thee four square--

Be ye at PEACE and POISE- and let nothing be unto thee a thorn in thy foot.

I say ye shall walk with surety at all times- ye shall not fall- neither shall ye falter-

So be it ye shall not be left alone- nor shall ye perish!

I say be ye at PEACE and POISE.

Blest shall ye be- I am come that ye might have peace- so be it and Selah.

Be ye as one which has my hand upon thee and I shall bless thee- so be it and Selah.

I am thy older Brother and thy Sibor- Sananda

Recorded by Sister Thedra of the Emerald Cross

"PRAISE HIM..." SORI SORI

Sori Sori -- Behold I am come -

I enter within thy temple - I come as thy guest -

I bless thee - I speak unto thee in accent sweet -

I prepare thee for the great communion of the Sons of God--

I bring unto thee sweet fragrance -

I come with the sword of TRUTH -

I bring the torch of freedom -

I place it within thy hand -

I speak unto thee that which the Father wills --

I give unto thee the key unto the KINGDOM of GLORY --

And the KING shall enter within the time which is near --

Praise the Father Mother God --

Lift up thine eyes - behold all things made new --

I come that all things may be made new - so be it and Selah.

Be ye as one made whole --

Praise ye O my soul --

Lift up thine eyes unto the heavens -

Bow down unto no man --

Hold high thine head -

Sing ye the PRAISE of Father Mother God which has given unto thee being --

Bless them which spite fully use thee --

Give unto thyself credit for being a son of God the Father --

Bless thee O my Soul -

Be ye eternally blest -

Call and ye shall be heard -

I shall serve thee diligently -

O my child PRAISE ye this day - IT IS COME! IT IS COME!

I say unto thee IT IS COME! Give unto the Father all the credit and the Glory--

Praise ye the name of SOLEN AUM SOLEN--

For I say unto thee he has given unto thee being and unto Him all the PRAISE AND THE GLORY --

SING YE LANDS OF THE EARTH!

HEAR ME ye PEOPLE of THE EARTH!

IT IS COME - when the waters shall be divided --

And the hills shall be leveled --

And the rains shall come --

And the winds shall blow --

And families shall be divided --

And fire and water shall mix --

And the torrents shall run uphill --

And the winds shall fan the fires --

And great destruction shall come upon the earth --

Yet I say unto thee: ALL THESE THINGS are but the beginning of the GLORIOUS NEW DAWN!

Be at PEACE - and give thanks that it is come!

I say that they which are privileged to partake of this time - this day - this age - are as ones blest forever - so be it and Selah.

Would ye not PROFIT for thy own sake?

I say be ye as one blessed for great shall be thy reward --

HOLY is HIS name - which ye shall remember - and speak --

PRAISE ye the name of SOLEN AUM SOLEN --

And keep it ever within thine heart - keep it holy and immaculate

Fear not - and walk ye with SURETY -- place thine hand in HIS.

Yield not unto temptation and ye shall be delivered up.

Praise ye all the days of thy LIFE - and be ye at PEACE --

Bring the labor of thy hands unto the altar of the most high LIVING GOD - and great shall be thy reward --

Blest shall ye be --

Bring thyself as a living sacrifice unto the altar --

And it shall be acceptable unto HIM the KING of GLORY --

And ye shall abide with HIM forever more --

Be ye at PEACE and POISE --

Blest be ye my child --

I am with thee unto the end --

I am known as one without end - without beginning --

I AM the ALPHA and the OMAGA --

I know myself to be - so AM I - So be it - Selah.

Sori Sori.

Recorded by Sister Thedra of the Emerald Cross

"Be ye responsible..."

Beloved of my being: I come unto thee this day that ye may be blest -- so be it and Selah.

I say ye shall be blest -- and I give unto thee this word for them that they too might be blest --

Be ye as ones prepared for the day which is now come --

And ye shall be as ones which have my hand upon thee -- and I shall bless thee -- and I shall lead thee into the place wherein I am.

And ye shall be glad for thy preparation - so be it and Selah.

I say ye shall walk with me - and talk with me - and ye shall be as one lifted up -- ye shall know no want - nor shall ye perish--

I say - it is my part to give unto thee the law -- and it is thy part to walk in the way set before thee--

Ye have not heard that which has been said -- therefore it is repeated over and over many times--and in many ways--that none might be found wanting--

So be it that I am come that they might all be spared the suffering which shall come upon the earth.

I am of a mind to deliver thee out--Yet I say ye shall do thy part - and alert thyself - and be unto thyself true - and force not thy responsibility upon another--

For it is the law EVERY MAN - WOMAN and CREATURE upon the earth is self-responsible --

And it is said over and over many times -- "Be ye as one responsible for thy own salvation--"

Ye are thy OWN SAVIOR - none other have ye - such is the law.

I say - there are no laggards in the house of the LORD --

So be it I have spoken. Amen so let it be --

I am Sananda

> **Recorded by Sister Thedra of the Emerald Cross**

Sananda - "I shall bring thee into the place of my abode...

Beloved of my being --blest are thou--and blest shall ye be--

I am come that ye may be blest--

I say unto thee--Ye shall be forever blest--for it is now come when ye shall walk and talk with me --and ye shall know me as I know thee - so be it and Selah.

I am the King of Glory and I shall bring thee into the place of my abode - wherein ye shall be as one born of HIM a SON of GOD- Wherein ye shall walk with HIM- and talk with HIM and wherein ye shall know as He knows--

I say ye shall inherit the KINGDOM of GOD--

I say there shall be no secrets from thee-

I say ye shall know as HE knows-such is thy inheritance--

I say ye have gone out from His place of abode and unto HIM ye shall return --

Praise the name of SOLEN AUM SOLEN - it is now come when ye shall be brought out of bondage -

So be it and Selah.

I am come that ye may be brought out this day--

When ye have set thy house in order- and when thy task is done.

I shall bring thee into the place wherein I am and

I shall give unto thee that which has been kept for thee--

I say unto thee ye shall be as one forever blest--

I say unto thee ye shall be as one which has earned thy freedom.

I say ye shall be as one brought out of bondage - forever free - so be it and Selah--

I say ye have gone out as one which has been given free will-

And ye have gone into the world of man of thy own free will

That they might be blest of me through thee -

So be it that ye have been unto thyself true - ye have been

Unto thy trust true - and now ye shall be as one free forever -

Forever free - So be it and Selah--

I say ye shall give this unto them and they shall bear witness of these my words unto thee-- and I use words which they shall comprehend--and I say they shall remember these my words which I say unto thee--they shall bear witness--and they shall remember MY WORDS--

There are none so foolish as the one which thinks himself wise- and none so sad as the one which betrays himself - or his trust - so be it and Selah. I am come that they may have LIGHT - and I work in ways they know not of -- I go into the realms they know not- I give unto them in ways they comprehend not--

I say they know me not--yet I am--and I KNOW MYSELF TO BE - so be it and Selah--I am with thee unto the end--

I AM--and I KNOW MYSELF TO BE--I AM Sananda Son of God - Amen and Selah.

Recorded by Sister Thedra of the Emerald Cross

Sananda - "Come abide with me in Peace"...

Beloved of my being--Be ye blest of me this day --draw nigh unto me and I shall speak unto thee--and ye shall give it unto them which are of a mind to hear that which I have said unto thee--

I say ye shall give unto them the privilege of hearing that which I have said unto thee- ye shall not deny them the privilege--

For it is long past time - that they have slept--they sleepeth still

And I say - they shall awaken--

And they shall be removed from the earth - for it is now the age when every living creature shall find a new abiding place -

And they shall be put into their own environment--and it shall behoove them to prepare them self for a greater part--a better environment--such is progress--I say: such is progress--and it is that which shall prosper them--

I say it is NOT worldly goods which prosper them - or makes of them SONS of GOD--

I say--they are the ones responsible for their own preparation - And none shall look unto another for his salvation--

I say - NOT ONE comes save of his own will and of his own effort-- And for his effort is he better--

Be ye blest this day - and say unto them as I now say unto thee- "ALERT THYSELF AND COME FORTH AS A SON OF THE ALMIGHTY GOD WHICH HAS GIVEN UNTO THEE BEING"

Praise His Name--and give thanks this day is come--

I say - when they lift up their hearts and when they seek their salvation from the source which has given unto them their being they shall be as ones lifted up--

They shall be as ones delivered out of bondage forever- for I say that it is the Father's will that all men be delivered up - so be it and Selah.

Be ye as ones on whose shoulders rests thy own salvation--

I am come that ye may have light--I say ye have walked in darkness lo eons of time - and now ye shall be given as ye are prepared to receive - and ye shall profit thereby.

I say that none shall force upon thee that which ye are not prepared to receive-- Be ye as ones blest to receive me and of me - for I am come that ye might have light - and that shall be unto thee all which is sufficient unto thy salvation--

It is my part to give unto thee the law - and it is thy part to abide by it - and to walk in the way set before thee - such is my word unto them - and be ye blest that ye have received me - so shall they likewise be blest--

I am thy sibor and thy Brother Sananda.

COME ABIDE WITH ME IN PEACE.

                Recorded by Sister Thedra of the Emerald Cross

FATHER ETERNAL - "Be ye no part of darkness..."

Beloved of my being - be ye as my hand and as my mouth unto them-- and say unto them in my name that there are none so foolish as the ones which think themself wise--

And give unto them this word: While they have slept the dragon has used them--he has gone the long way to cause to sleep --

He has given unto them the part which has caused them to sleep --

He has tormented them --

He has held them in bondage --

He has given unto them the portion which he has fortuned out for them and they have accepted it - and asked of him MORE ---

I say they have not the mind to ask of me - the giver of all GOOD and TRUE SUBSTANCE --

They have not the strength of their own to stand as the PILLAR of LIGHT which they are--and hey know it not--

I say they know it not--Be ye blest this day - and stand as the EVERLASTING SYMBOL OF MAN which I have willed thee to be—

Weep not for them which misuse thee--give unto them naught which they can use against thee--and bless them with thy whole being - and give unto them the part which shall be given unto thee for them-

And be ye not concerned what they say or do - for it is their own doing - and their own responsibility-- I shall not ask of thee an accounting for them--for there is NONE which shall be held accountable for the actions and the motives of another--

Be ye as one responsible for thy own deeds - thy own part -

And be ye as one which has been brought out from among them-

And be ye no part of their darkness--their foolishness--so be it that they shall arouse themself in due season--and I shall receive them as the year which brings forth its harvest--all things unto its season--

Be ye as one prepared to be brought in - for it is now come when great and GLORIOUS LIGHT shall flood the earth -

And the power of the LIGHT shall be more than they can bear - -

And they shall remove themself from the earth by law - which is the law of LIFE - and LIGHT--and no man shall resist it for it knows not change, and for this do they go and come --

Yet I say unto thee they have no comprehension of the LAW of LIFE--

They put upon it their own interpretations--they give unto the law credit for that which they do of their own WONTON –

They offer up their puny sacrifices--they go unto their priests which have ordained themself-which have not the love of GOD within them-- They give them self credit for being wise - when they ask of man forgiveness--and they counsel not with me!

I say they know me not! And they are not of a mind to accept my emissaries which I send out- for they have martyred my prophets- and crucified my SON-- I say--they cut themself off from me –

I am within the place where in I am as one prepared to receive them when they turn unto me--and bring unto me themself as a living sacrifice- and give unto me their HEART - HANDS - and their WILL - which I have endowed unto them--

I shall not trespass upon their will for I have given it freely-- and freely shall I accept it--and in turn I shall receive them unto myself--

In the end I shall BE - and I AM without beginning - I AM without end-- I AM -- I AM - thy FATHER ETERNAL -

Spoken -- SOLEN - SOLEN - AUM SOLEN

Beloved of my being : be ye blest this day - and be ye as my hand and my mouth made manifest unto them which are of a mind to receive me and of me - and I shall bless thee -- And I shall reveal unto them which do receive my words that which has been hidden from them --

I shall give unto them that for which they have waited-- For it is now come when there shall be great changes - and when many shall be removed from the earth by natural law--and they shall be put into a place provided for them - and they shall be as ones which have created their own environment - wherein they shall awaken--

I say it behooves them to prepare themself this day - for pity are they which betray themself--

I am one sent of GOD the FATHER that they be prepared - so be it that I shall be true unto my trust - and they shall be as ones which have been given a free will--and I shall not trespass upon it.

And they shall be responsible for their own actions and for their choice--For none shall be responsible for them--so be it that I am the Way Shower and I can by law but point the way - so be it that there are none which can bear the responsibility of another's sin or UNKNOWING -- the result of their "UN-KNOWING" - the result of their actions--

I say none can accept the responsibility of the salvation of another - so be it that I am the one sent of God the Father that there might be LIGHT - and they either accept it or reject it - and be unto themself traitor.. Blest are they which accept the LIGHT which I bring-- Mighty is the LAW - and swift is the sword of TRUTH - and the reaper grim--

I speak plainly and with the power of God - for I speak of the law which they know not - and they know me not which go into the dens of the porcupines for Light -- I say they know me not!

I speak unto thee that they might have truth - and they look for signs and wonders - they seek phenomena -- they look for miracles and they see not the hand of God move in the winds - and the waves - they see not the beauty of the snowflake - the rain droplets - they see not the SPIRIT of GOD move as man made manifest--

They give unto themself credit for being wise--and they cry out from oppression--yet they look afar - and they see not that which is nearer than hand and foot--

They know not that the Father has breathed the WORD which has given unto them being - and they have not been of a mind to turn unto HIM in ADORATION that they might GLORIFY HIM in the earth - and that they might be lifted up--so be it and Selah.

I come that they all might be lifted up -- so be it and Selah.

I am the Son of God - known herein as Sananda.

Recorded by Sister Thedra of the Emerald Cross

Sananda - "There are ones which do come to scatter and divide..."

Beloved of my being: Ye shall be blest this day--and ye shall walk and talk with me --

Ye shall now say unto them in my name that it is finished--it is done!

And ye shall add unto that - that there are none so sad as the ones which betray themself--

I say - that wherein I am there are no traitors!

I am not so foolish as to sibor traitors --

I give not the foolish the pearls of great price - so be it I am as one which knows them - and I see that which they do - and I find their in-most secrets--for there is nothing hidden from me ---

So be it that they which do spit upon my words and set foot against my prophets shall be accountable unto the law--for it is the law--

When they give unto themself credit for being wise - I say the law is sure and swift - such is JUSTICE METED OUT by the <u>LAW of JUSTICE</u> which is eternal and which was in the beginning - and no man shall change it--

Yet every man is accountable for his own part - his own actions - and the law which he sets into motion of his own free will--

I am not the maker of the law - yet I abide by it--I create not that which shall torment me - I give not that which I do not want --

I care not for their opinions - nor for their coin - for I am sufficient unto myself - and I care for my own - and I bless myself for I know myself to be one with the SOURCE of all blessing-all GOOD --

I give unto them which serve me as I receive of God the Father--for I am sent that they might be lifted up--yet I say when they set themself up - and when they give unto themself credit for being wise - PITY ARE THEY - for they are the greatest of fools--

So be it that I DO WEEP for them! It has been said that I am a man of sorrows - such are my sorrows - so be it and Selah.

I am now come unto thee that they might have these my words--and I command thee- give them unto them which are of a mind to receive them-

And say unto them in my name that there are ones which do walk among them which are of darkness - that which they know not of - which do come to scatter and divide - and which are sent from out the den of the dragon--

And I say too - likewise are the ones sent of God the Father to deliver them up - to rescue them from the snare of the FOWLER - and he which would snare them is but the one which is of the DRAGON sent. He has many plans - should one fail he resorts unto yet more ruthless ones - so be it and Selah.

I am of a mind to cast them into utter darkness-- Yet I say the LAW is SWIFT as the two-edged SWORD and the fortune of them which do fall under the yolk of the dragon is sad indeed--so be it and Selah. I command thee give this unto them at the earliest possible time so be it they shall bear witness of these my words - so be it and Selah--

I am thy brother - and thy sibor - Son of God the Father known as Sananda --

Recorded as spoken By Sister Thedra of the Emerald Cross

Ye have stood as rocks- and through the strength you gave forth the condition in Mt. Shasta was more quickly worked out than it could have been had you wavered and lost faith. Many more difficult tests will meet thy Sibors- and weak indeed would we be had we failed in the slight stumbling blocks in our path. It seems great to thee but we are not moved--we will face many greater tests before the new age is established.

Now you will go on - stronger than before because of thy faith and strength in passing through this small rough place on to attainment. Each one has learned a valuable lesson- and this is good for thee and for thy Sibors- what strengthens thee helps all and all are blest.

Great changes are coming for all- for this ye must be prepared Ye have asked to serve as needed and according to thy development-- there is to be no square pegs in round holes-- all must work smoothly---

No more are we to be used as testing grounds for those unprepared for the work they choose to do-another will be found to show them their weaknesses-- and less time will be lost---

All must discover and know their weakness for all must have the chance to prove themself-- They had earned their chance and it was given unto them-- shall they be--

Blest shall ye be for thy faith and strength.

Thy Sibor- Orlando.

Recorded by Sorea Sorea.

Sananda Speaking to Sorea Sorea:

We who walk unseen among thee are not deceived by appearances. We read the heart of such one- and know the true nature of thy being- thy dreams and thy frustrations- thy anxieties and fears.

Can we not lead thee and guide and be unto thee succor in all times of need? Put thy trust in thy Sibors and know according to thy trust and faith- no harm shall come nigh thy door-- when thou hast learned the truth of all things ye will laugh at all thy fears-- and know the nothingness of worldly wisdom--

Man walks in utter darkness for the most part- and knows not of the great inner plan - the wonderful plan for all life- nothing is ever lost from the Fathers sight.

Prepare ye for the coming great age- ye shall prepare thyself lest ye spend long ages groping in the dark as ye have done in the past-- SO AGONIZING- SO MOURNFUL!

Is it not TIME ye grew to thy full estate and abide in Peace and Joy forever?

Ye have but to desire and ask and <u>obey</u> the Fathers will -- walk as He would have ye walk and ye will see Him face to face.

Great will be the rejoicing in the Fathers house- be ye not afraid- ye will not be led astray- ye will walk in certainty and with much joy--be ye not afraid.

I leave thee with this assurance- ye walk not alone- I am with thee always--

As I say unto thee I say unto all.

I am thy older Brother - Sananda.

Sori Sori:- Beloved of my being be ye blest of me and by me- and give unto me credit for being that which I am-- and sing PRAISE- and give thanks unto the Father Mother God that they have sent thee forth at this time to bear witness of these things--

I say that these are the days for which we have waited- and I am glad it is come when we do have this privilege of communication- and this concourse--

For I am with thee- and I shall be with thee at the end--for I come that ye may be brought out of bondage- so be it and selah.

I am thy Sibor and Benefactor.   Sori Sori.

Recorded by Sister Thedra of the Emerald Cross

Blessings upon thee my child-- walk with me through the sunlit paths- wherein there is peace and serenity--

I come unto thee that ye may know peace such as thou has not known ---

Blest am I that I am permitted by law to come unto thee- for this have I waited--

I say unto thee I walk hand in hand with my beloved brother whom we know as Sananda the Lord Jesus Christ of our world/yours and mine--

I say unto thee My Beloved of whom I speak fondly I call thee MY CHILD- for I have watched thee-- I have cherished the memory of our time together- when we walked hand in hand through the Elesian fields wherein we shared the great joy of our being ONE within the great temple of the SUN--

Wherein we knew the law governing the things which now you are struggling so hard to remember-- and because of thy remembering your longing has been greater--

Yet thy memory remains clouded by the veil of Maya---

Beloved I say unto thee thy memory shall be restored-- ye shall remember--and I am GLAD! So be it a great day - and glad shall ye be--

I say unto thee you and I shall again walk the sun-lit path of the long forgotten temple grounds wherein we last met-- and ye shall be glad it is finished- so be it and Selah.

I am thy long forgotten Brother--Sorica.

Recorded by Thedra

Sarah speaking--Beloved of my being- be ye blest of me and by me and glad ye shall be- for I come that ye may be blest- and so shall ye be---

Sori Sori- shall give unto thee a part separate and apart from this and ye shall be as one prepared to receive it- so shall it be given unto them which are prepared to receive it/ all which are of a mind to receive of him and by him- such is his part to give unto them of his love and energy---

And when they do receive of him they shall profit thereby so be it and Selah.

* * *

Sori Sori- I come as - Sori- and I speak as Sori--and as such I go-- for I am that-- I come with no effort - for I am one with the Father Mother God and I am not apart- nor do I separate from them---

I move upon the deep--I go within the earth--

I was- and I am the GOD of the wind- of the rain-- and of the lightning--

I go not neither do I come--

I AM---

And I am not moved by thy opinions- nor thy wonton--

I pre-see that which is to be--for I see all that is- and has been- all that shall be---

I am the one which was sent forth as the custodian of the elements which was given into my custody from the beginning---

I am the keeper of the key-- and they obey --and the elements are but my hand maid--

I sing and the wind dances--

I write and the ethers record my writing upon the everlasting tablets of timeless substance---

I sing and the winds pick up my anthems- and they which have ears to hear- hear that which I send forth for them

I say I am the keeper of the KEYS unto the secrets of the elements---

I give unto thee the key--

I speak unto thee as Sori Sori Born of GOD am I- the keeper of the keys--

I speak unto thee as such- and ye shall be entrusted with my GIFT for I am of a mind to bestow my gift upon thee--

For I say unto thee ye have used thy gifts wisely and justly-- And ye have been as one found trustworthy-- such is my part to give unto thee this part- and ye shall receive this part as my gift endowed unto me of GOD the FATHER which has favored me above all other with this office---

I say I am the one favored to be the keeper of the keys--so on thee I bestow MY GIFT as my privilege- and as my right- by divine inheritance-

I give unto thee MY MANTLE- MY SHIELD- and MY GIFT unto thee- So be it in the name of the MOST HIGH LIVING GOD- Amen and SELAH.

I am thy benefactor and thy brother--

Sori Sori Son of God am I- and I speak as man- and in language which ye comprehend--I give unto thee the keys unto the KINGDOM of EARTH- and the elements there of- so shall ye accept them in the name of the Father MOTHER GOD- and by their GRACE ye shall accept that which is willed unto thee of them from the beginning- so be it and Selah

Come with me and be ye free from all bondage - forever free--- And I say unto thee NO more shall ye be bound by the earth and the elements thereof- so be it and Selah.

I give unto thee my CLOAK of AUTHORITY/ MY MANTLE- and MY SHIELD so be it thy security- and THY SHIED and BUCKLER in the time of need so be it and Selah---

I come that this may be accomplished and so shall it be Amen and Selah.

I say ye shall place this upon the altar for a time - and then it shall be sent unto them which have the mind to comprehend - and they shall bear witness of my words unto thee- for ye shall work with the elements--and they shall be thy hand maidens-- and they shall serve thee faithfully and lovingly- such is my word for thy day--and I have spoken- and thou hast heard me-so be it according to the Fathers will--I abide by it- so be it and Selah--

I am Sori Son of God So be it.

Recorded by Sister Thedra of the Emerald Cross

Sori Sori -- Blest art thou this day -- and blest shall ye be.

Ye shall now say unto them in my name that I am one upon whose shoulders rest the responsibility of the winds and the waters and the elements of fire.

I give unto them that which should give unto them comfort - yet they know me not--nor do they ask of me--the giver of the goodly part--

They seek within their own limited world that which should enable them to conquer the elements--and it shall be said herein that the elements are NOT CONQUERED -- for they are the fortune of God the Father and obey the law--even as HIS SONS do obey the law--

I say the elements shall obey the law of LOVE and be unto thee thy willing and obedient handmaid - for the law shall govern all things and ye shall be as ones obedient unto it OR ye shall be as ones which set into motion which is the reverse of LOVE -- and that shall be unto thee thy own downfall --

I say ye shall be obedient unto the law--or it shall consume thee--such is the power of the LAW!

Blest are they which serve thee in LOVE and in Peace shall he reign -- so be it and Selah. I am with thee that ye may learn of me and for this have I spoken of this law of LOVE--and the reverse--which is man's wonton--his own work--his own bearing. He has turned his face from GOD the Father--and he tries to mock Him -- I say God is <u>not</u> mocked--for it is the foolishness of fools. So be it and Selah.

Mighty and unerring is the LAW!

And for that we which do keep it are glad--for we weary not in our appointed tasks--we sleep not--neither do we go out from our place of abode. We keep constant watch--yet there are ones which do go out and which have done so that ye may be confused and tormented--so be it that they are not sent of the Father that ye might be comforted--

They are as ones sent of the Dragon that ye might be held in bondage.

I say the Dragon is NOT OF A MIND to unleash thee--so be it that we which are sent come that ye may be freed from all bounds--therefore we speak thusly--that ye shall have such knowledge as which will free thee in LOVE and OBEDIENCE with the LAW--

The word is but the reminder--and all whosoever receives the word/the reminder unto himself shall find the truth thereof for he shall be sibored from the realms of light--such is the law of the ONE ALMIGHTY GOD FATHER MOTHER - which has brought us forth in this time and for all eternity shall we ever be one in them--in the ONE which shall endure-- which is without beginning and without end. So be it and Selah.

I am with thee that ye might know thy ONENESS and be ye conscious of it by day and by night--walk ye in the LIGHT.

I am SORI SORI

Recorded by Sister Thedra of the Emerald Cross

Beloved of my Being:- I come unto thee this day for the purpose of giving unto thee this word- and ye shall give it unto them and they shall be as ones prepared to receive it for it is now come when many shall turn unto the light and for this are we prepared---

Say unto them as I would say that we thy brothers of light stand ready to give unto them as they are prepared to receive-- and when they have accepted us and the plan which is now prepared and given unto us for thee- we shall be as ones glad to step forth and reveal unto thee- unto them which have been prepared for such revelation this plan which has been revealed unto us from the Fathers own hands--

I say we are now prepared to step forth as thy older brothers which have gone before thee to prepare the way- such is our part. And it is thy part to prepare thyself to receive us and ye shall be glad- for we have gone the long way to bless thee--

And we are of the Father sent- and ye shall come to know that which is hidden from thee so be it and Selah.

By thy own effort shall ye be prepared- and ye shall be diligent in thy preparation- and ye shall not turn aside- nor shall ye falter--

Ye shall abide in me- and I shall bring thee out of bondage-- and I am sent that ye might be free-forever free--yet ye shall accept me for that which I am- and I shall come in and abide with thee- and I shall counsel thee and ye shall learn of the WILL of the FATHER MOTHER GOD- so be it and Selah.

I am with thee- and I shall reveal myself when ye are so prepared so be it and Selah.

Sananda Son of God- known as Jesus

Christ son of Mary- the ward of Joseph, so be it and selah.

Recorded by Sister Thedra of the Emerald Cross

Bor speaking:- Be ye blest this day- and I shall speak unto thee of the ETHICS of SPEECH-

I say that there are few which know that which is ethical- and what is prompted by love---

I say few indeed speak ethically- and few serve the forces of light- for one has but to observe the humanity which does exist within the earth- and upon it--

And I say they speak that which is prompted by the forces of darkness- and they bring about their own confusion- and they are as ones which have bound themself in darkness---

So be it that they shall come to know the power of the spoken word- and for that am I glad--I come that they may be given such comprehension so be it and Selah.

I say this is my part that they come to know what is meant by ethics- and it is no small task- for they have fortuned unto themself their own opinions and their own part which they cling to so tenaciously---

When they learn the foolishness of their own opinions and their own ideas and seek the light they shall be given great revelation so be it and Selah.

Ye shall go unto them and say that which shall be given unto thee to say- and they shall hear the words which shall come out of thy mouth--and they shall be as ones wise to heed them- for the Father shall put words into thy mouth and they shall be HIS words- and they shall not deny HIM for he shall be as thy POWER- thy LIFE- thy SALVATION-

And ye shall glorify HIM on the earth- and ye shall be unto thyself true and ye shall speak with authority and with power- for He shall be unto thee all that which is necessary so be it and Selah.

I am now prepared to give unto thee another part of the Book of DISCIPLINE- and I say ye shall return at a later hour for to record it-- and it shall be a new part- so be it and Selah.

Ye shall give this unto them- and it shall be added unto the Temple Scripts- so let it go on record as my part--

I am come that they may know me and my part shall be revealed unto them--

I am not a popular one-- for I am the Father of DISCIPLINE and I am now prepared to give them the part which is the extreme and ultimate tests-- for wherein is it said: "THERE SHALL BE TRYING TIMES AHEAD"

I endeavor to prepare them to meet these things- and to MASTER such situations as they shall encounter---

I say there are none so foolish as the one which thinks himself wise- and none so sad as the one which betrays himself - so be it he is the saddest of the lot---

I see them and know them for that which they are- and I stand ready to sibor them - that they be free forever -- such is my part- and it is their part to accept the responsibility of their own preparation-- and to prepare themself in the time allotted unto them so be it the better part of wisdom---

I am thy Sibor and thy Brother- Bor

Recorded by Thedra of the Emerald Cross.

Sananda speaking unto those who have a mind to hear:

The short time ye have yet to use- must be used for the work of the Hierarchy. Not a moment must ye waste- ye must ever be about thy Fathers business.

This is not the time for idleness or wasted energy- misused energy is forever lost to the work at hand- be ye ever mindful of this- thy Sibors work continuously for the fulfillment of the plan- can ye not do thy part?

This is not for the few who are doing all their human natures permit- but for those who sleep or play along the way- so willing for others to do the work. YE LAGGARDS- ye shall find thyself crying at the gate- and it closed and locked- for another long age.

AWAKEN AND REPENT! Ye shall be about thy Fathers business. This warning I give in LOVE- knowing as ye do not- the terrible consequences of thy disobedience.

I say this- I say that-- ever trying to say that which will awaken thee to thy impending peril- if ye do not awaken and stir thyself to aid thy Sibors.

BE YE ALERT!- let not the bridegroom come and find thy lamp unlit- for He cometh when ye know not.

BE FOREVER WATCHFUL- I am the good shepherd- I watch over My Sheep- but when the time cometh all must be ready- lest the wolf catch one unaware-- ye must keep thy attention upon the shepherd- and be aware of HIM- that He may warn thee in time.

I am ever mindful of thee- ye must do thy part- it is the law- it cannot be done for thee.

I come to claim my own- ye must choose- I do not choose who will follow me- and so I await thy call.

BE QUICK!

I am thy Sibor and Elder Brother, Sananda.

Recorded by Sorea Sorea

Blest art thou Oh my child- be ye filled with joy this day- and give unto them this my word unto them--

And they shall be reminded of me by day and by night-- for I am come that they might know me- and that they might be prepared for to receive me--

For thou art my hand made manifest unto them that they might begin to stir within their slumbers - and I say they shall awaken and they shall bring forth fruit which shall be acceptable unto the Father Mother God-- and unto Him all the praise and the glory--

I am that which has come forth that they may awaken from their sleep- and they have slept overtime--

Now there shall be a great voice ring out which shall awaken them- then they shall hear it- and the ones which do not awaken shall be removed from the earth forever- and they shall be put in the place which is prepared for them and they shall be as the traitors unto themself -for they shall begin anew---

And the ones which do awaken- and accept their divine inheritance shall be as the Sons of God the Father- and they shall inherit the earth- and they shall be the keepers of the records thereof- for I say the earth shall move out into her new place of abode wherein she shall be free from the torment which she goes through at this time---

I say she is tormented- for she is enmeshed within the folds of the great and powerful goat which has come into being in the <u>last century</u> - it is not a goat as you speak of it- it is a great part of the O cycle in which the earth travels- and wherein she shall enter into another - which is likened unto a water jug filled with water- when it is forced from the bottom/ topside down- and wherein there is little air--

The earth has been forced from its place wherein she would have her equilibrium and her proper balance- now she reels and rocks as a drunkard---

And it is my part to stand guard- that she does not faint and perish- I say I am alert- and mindful of my part- and I shall not betray my trust- for I am given this part of GOD MY FATHER - and I am glad---

So be it that I serve with great joy! and for to glorify Him and I am not of a mind to betray myself/ nor my trust- so be it that I come that they might be reminded of me- and of my part- and that they might be about their preparation- such is wisdom---

I speak as one which has come for this purpose/ that they might be spared much suffering--

I say- AWAKEN ALL YE NATIONS OF THE EARTH- PRAISE YE THE FATHER WHICH HAS GIVEN UNTO THEE BEING- BLEST SHALL YE BE. I am Gabriel.

Recorded by Sister Thedra of the Emerald Cross

Beloved of my being:- Be ye as my hand made manifest this day and I do declare for thee thy freedom from all bondage forever.

I say unto thee ye shall be free forever- so be it and Selah---

I say unto them which are as yet in bondage that it is now come when great changes shall come about - and so swiftly that they shall stand amazed- and confounded-- and they shall cry out from fright--while the ones which are prepared shall cry out from sheer joy for the privilege of being part of this great age- the transition of earth and MAN---

I do declare for the earth her liberation from bondage-- for the Father has willed that all living things shall be free--so be it that man has caused his own suffering- and he has been his own tormentor-- he has accepted his own downfall as final--

He has gone out from the Father free- and he has the will to use - for his own return-- and the law is clearly stated- and recorded -- and when he is so minded that he so chooses to obey and abide by the law he shall be as one free forever---

And the Father shall receive him unto himself so be it a glad day--I say glad shall he be-- Amen and Selah. I am the Son of God and the one born of Mary- ward of Joseph so be it and Selah.

Recorded by Sister Thedra of the Emerald Cross

LITERAL TRANSLATION

of

THE LORD'S PRAYER

as said by

THE MASTER

Given by the Lord Mikaal*

"Our Father who dwells in Heaven,

"Glorified be Your Name,

"Your Kingdom come into the World, as it does in Spirit.

"Give to us this day that which we need for our sustenance.

"Forgive us that which we do in err as we forgive those who err against us. "

* * *

We are indebted to:

THE LODGE OF THE SILVER LEAF

OF THE WHITE BROTHERHOOD,

THE GROUP OF SOLAR TEACHING.

Arch Angel Michael/Prince Michael

Beloved of my being: - be ye blest of me and by me. I come that ye may be blest-- I give unto thee this part for them which are of a mind to receive it--and it shall not be forced upon any one-- and as they receive so shall they give---

Ye shall be unto them my hand made manifest- and they shall be glad for my part- and likewise they shall remember my servants for I shall give unto thee that which they shall remember in the days ahead---

I say, I give unto none foolish parts/or foolish sayings--- I am as one prepared to give unto them as they are prepared to receive-- and they which do accept that which I say unto them shall be as ones prepared for the greater part--

And I do not give my pearls unto babes which do not know their worth---I say ye shall be as one which has my hand upon thee and ye shall be blest of me-and by me-- and in turn ye shall be my hand made manifest unto them-yet ye shall not be unto them the scapegoat---

Ye shall walk with dignity- and ye shall hold high thy head- and ye shall not grovel for a pittance--

And they shall be unto themself/ self-sustaining and they which do receive of this my work shall be as ones which have the responsibility of their part of the load---

I say that none shall place all the responsibility of this work upon another-- yet each unto his part--ye shall be as my hand made manifest unto them-- and they shall be as my hand made manifest unto thee- for they shall sustain thee- and give unto thee that which is necessary that my hands be free- for this work at the altar---

And I say unto thee woe unto any man or woman which so ever that desecrates this my work--or misuses it in any manner whatsoever---

I am now prepared to come unto any one where ever they might be who so ever accepts my words- and to sibor them in my ways - as the Father has willed it-

And I pray ye that they might all turn their face unto the light.

I am with thee unto the end--

Recorded by Sister Thedra

The "Sleepers."

"Beloved: Ye shall say unto them:- The time is short and there are few laborers in the vineyard- and it is necessary each do his part; that the load is indeed heavy- and the servants are few--

When they are prepared for the next part they shall make it known unto this office and the next part- or portion- will be sent unto them...

And for this shall they receive as it is given- and not one word shall be changed--such is my word unto them through thee- such shall they have- and it shall profit them- for these parts have been blest- and they which take them unto themself shall be blest so be it and Selah"

Sananda: We the servants add our Love and labor that you may be blest by God the Father Mother through us. It is our joy to serve.

Fraternally Thedra

Berea speaking: blest of my being; I come unto thee that they may have these MY WORDS---

And I say unto them- there is little while left in which they may come unto the altar- for it is near unto the time when the gate shall be closed--

And they shall stand as ones forsaken- for it is now come when the ones which hold out a hand shall move on into other fields- and ye shall be as ones wise indeed to meet the day with these words:

"Father, I wait NO MORE- I come unto thee and NO FALSE GODS shall I have before thee--

I shall be unto myself true- and I shall go into the secret place wherein thou abidest- and I shall counsel with THEE--

I know Thou shall not turn me away--

I ask of thee Oh Almighty Father other God- -

Give unto me strength and wisdom to discern the TRUE from the false---

I ask of thee - be my hand and my foot- for Thou hast given unto me being- and no other God shall I adore --

Behold ME THY CHILD- I COME--

I give unto thee all PRAISE and the GLORY forever--and forever--

I AM- for I KNOW that I AM-

And I PRAISE the OH FATHER- I PRAISE thee forever!"

Call with thine heart and He shall hear thee and give unto thee as ye are prepared to receive---

I am thy elder brother and thy guardian who has so loved thee that I wait- I wait with longing for thy return---

Bless thee my own beloved sister - my hand made manifest unto them---

Berea.

Recorded by Sister Thedra of the Emerald Cross

Beloved of my being:- blest art thou and blest shall ye be- I come that ye may be blest --

When I am come unto thee it is because of thy preparation- and ye have so prepared thyself that ye might receive me - and I am glad.

Now ye shall say unto them - as I would say that there are many among them which are prepared to give unto them the waters of Life and they shall prepare themself for to receive it/ the substance of LIFE- from which all things perfect are made---

Now when ye are prepared ye shall drink of the water of LIFE -- and ye shall step forth from thy body of dense flesh into thy HOLY CHRIST body as one perfect---

And I say unto thee- ye shall not taste of death- so be it and Selah.

I come that ye night have thy inheritance given unto thee of God the Father Mother/ cause of thy being---

Blest are they which receive it in full. I come -- as one which has received mine- and no man shall make me a pauper-- Nor shall he take from me mine inheritance- so be it and selah.

I am glad this day is come when I can speak unto thee as one be being unto another--

I am glad for my part- that ye might be brought out of bondage and so be it. Know ye this: as ye are prepared so shall ye receive-- I am thy Sibor known as "THE WAYSHOWER" and I have gone before before thee to prepare the way--so walk ye in it- and ye shall be glad forever more---

I shall lead thee into fertile pastures wherein ye shall hunger and thirst no more---

I am the Son of God-which ye know not yet --ye have given me names- - I am called Jesus of Nazereth- and I am now called Sananda Son of God wherein I am---

Recorded by Sister Thedra, of the Emerald Cross

EASTER SUNDAY

Beloved of my being:-

Blest art thou and blest shall ye be--I come that ye may be blest.

I speak unto thee that '<u>they</u> may have these words' and for them are they given unto thee-- ye shall be as one blest for this thy service unto the light of the Christ--

I say not one servant goes without reward- for they are that which goes in and out of the dark places to carry the light of the Christ--

It is the servants which are so necessary unto us thy Sibors- and without thee our servants - we are helpless- therefore I say- Blest are the servants- and they shall be blest for they shall be as ones rewarded of the Father Mother God--

Now it is come when they shall awaken- and they shall be as ones which have slept overtime- for much has gone on/been accomplished/ while they have slept- and they are as ones bound in darkness and they know not that which has been accomplished.

I say they are blind unto the light- and they see not- for the light blinds them while they sleepeth- yet when they awaken they shall see- and they will know that which they see- so be it a glad awakening--

I am glad it is now come when they shall awaken- for this have I waited- I say I have waited long for them which the Father has given unto me- for this do I give thanks unto HIM-ALMIGHTY-ALL WISE and GRACIOUS FATHER MOTHER GOD--

I give thanks this day- bless them which thou hast given into my care- I AM thy SON which thou hast sent forth for to bring them home--so be it that I shall be unto my trust true- and I shall not forsake them nor shall I betray them nor myself- so be it and Selah.

Blest am I O MY FATHER MOTHER that Thou hast given me being - of THYSELF have I come into being- and I am glad- O ALMIGHTY GOD- I do give unto thee ALL THE POWER and the GLORY forever!

Let thy LIGHT be made manifest upon the earth in every living spirit- that all darkness may be dispelled from the earth - forever and forever- Amen and Selah--

I am come that all darkness might be dispelled- so be it HALLAJULIA- GLORY unto HIM- and PRAISE HIS HOLY NAME. Son of God Sananda.

Recorded by Sister Thedra of the Emerald Cross

John The Beloved

Beloved I speak unto thee this day- as one come unto thee for the purpose of giving thee this portion for them--

And it shall be given unto them as it is received- and not one word shall be changed for it is given for a purpose- which shall be revealed unto them in due time--

Ye shall be as my hand made manifest unto them- and they shall remember thee- and give unto thee credit for being my hand made manifest - for without thy hand I could not reach them--

I speak unto them through thee- and ye shall be my mouth and my voice- for I come that ye may be my voice unto them--

Wherein is it said that ye shall have a new part?

So be it - and so shall it be--ye shall be unto them all that the Father would have thee be- and blest shall ye be---

Say unto them as I would say- that one shall go out from the Father as He- as the Father HIMSELF- and he shall be as one sent of the Father that there may be light within the earth sufficient to lift her up into the realms of light- wherein she shall be liberated from all darkness forever--

I say it is now come when all darkness shall be removed from the earth- and she shall be cleansed forever- and she shall not go into darkness no more---

There are now many within the earth for this part- yet it is near time when one which is to come shall walk upon the earth as flesh made manifest--

And I say unto thee it is true that the one known unto thee as Jesus the Christ is now upon the earth made flesh-- and he walketh as man- and he has within his hand the power to bring the out of bondage- when ye give unto him the power and the authority for ye have been given free will- and ye shall will it so- so be it as ye will it.

I speak unto thee simply and in terms ye may comprehend-- yet ye are of many minds- many opinions- and ye have the concept of man- NOT the MIND of GOD--

I say ye shall see with the EYE of GOD- ye shall have the mind which is of him--ye shall not be divided against thyself ye war within thyself- for ye are filled with many opinions of other minds- which is not of God the Father Mother--

I ask of thee be ye not divided against HIM which has given unto thee being--

I say be ye one with HIM- ask of HIM thy freedom-- and seek knowledge of HIM- and HE shall give unto thee that which shall profit thee---

Be ye blest of me and by me- for these my words carry with them the power and authority of God the Father- and ye shall be as one prepared to receive the greater part- so be it and Selah--

Praise ye the Father Mother God--unto HIM all the Glory---

I am sent of HIM that ye may come to know HIM in all HIS glory--

I am the Son called John the Beloved- so be it and so shall it be ye too are loved.

Recorded by Sister Thedra of the Emerald Cross

Sarah speaking: Beloved of my being-- blest art thou and blest shall ye be-- I come unto thee that ye may have this my word that which ye shall give unto them--

That they may know that which I say unto thee--and as much as I say it unto thee I say it unto them- for are they not mine- - have they not gone out from me as my breath made manifest?

And I say they are now preparing themself for their new abodes some shall remain with the earth until the last hour- then they which are the remnant shall be lifted up- even as the lamb is lifted up--

And I say- the ones which are not of the remnant shall go on to their new places which are prepared for them- and they shall be in their own environment and they shall be as ones prepared for their places- each unto his own- and they shall be as ones which have builded for himself his own dwelling place- for this I speak unto them- that they may be about their preparation-

For it is now come when they shall be alert and about their work which shall be that of preparation- such is their WORK.. I say they shall not waste the energy allotted unto them in idleness- and in waywardness- for therein is the folly of fools

I say it is given unto the foolish to have foolish ways--

I am not of a mind to reveal myself unto them--

Yet when they prepare themself I shall speak unto them so softly and gently- yet firmly- that they be not misled- for I am a watchful Mother and I speak as one with authority- and I am given unto wisdom and mercy so be it I am alert unto thy weakness and I shall be unto the parent/protector- and the ever loving MOTHER GOD from which thou hast gone out- -

So be it I shall await thy return with great patience and anticipation such is my part-- I am with thee unto the end-- I am they Mother Eternal-- Sarah.

Recorded by Sister Thedra of the Emerald Cross

The one to come: by GABRIEL

Beloved of my being:- be ye as my hand made manifest unto them and say unto them; that, in the time which is near one shall go out from the place wherein I am- and he shall walk among them as man- and he shall be as one with the Father Mother God-

I say he shall not separate himself from HIM- for he shall be as the Father made flesh- such is the will of God the Father--

I say he shall walk among thee- and he shall be as man- and be as God the Father made flesh--

He shall be born of woman- and yet he shall not be of the seed of man- for he shall be born of the Father--and even as Sananda/Jesus Christ-thy Lord--

He shall be born of earth mother- and of the Father impregnated of LIGHT substances--

I say he shall be as one born in the place now prepared for to receive him--and at the age of twelve years he shall go out from the cloistered place of his birth as man- of six foot- and a perfect stature-- he shall walk as a Son of God-- and he shall claim nothing of himself- he shall give unto the Father all credit and the glory--he shall do the Fathers will in ALL things- he shall walk as one born on wings--he shall bring unto him all them which are prepared--and unto them he shall give a sign- and a plan--and for this has he been granted this by the Father--

He shall gather together the ones which shall make up the remnant- and he shall give unto each a part and they shall be instructed in that part- and there shall be no laggards- no drunkards--for each shall be as ones balanced in all things--

And they shall be obedient in ALL THINGS- they shall be as ones blest --and I say ye shall live to see the day of his birth--

And yet few shall be as ones WISE- for few there shall be which shall know of his birth- at the time of his coming--and of his going all shall know-- for it is then that every eye shall behold his glory--

And every tongue shall sing his praise--every eye shall see him and behold him in all his glory--

And I say unto thee- that he shall bring with him a host which shall attend him--and they shall be unto him his right hand- for there shall be a multitude which shall be attended- and none shall be turned away--

And the curious shall be confused- and confounded- and they shall be as the foolish ones--for they shall not be satisfied- such is my word for them at this time-- I shall speak again that they might be prepared-so be it and Selah.

I am Gabriel.

Recorded by Sister Thedra of the Emerald Cross

Beloved of my being:- be ye as my hand made manifest unto them- say unto them as I would - that there are many among them which stand ready to relieve them from their stress and strain.

Yet- they are as yet not prepared to receive these benefactors which have come so lovingly and of their own free will- I say they shall be of a mind to receive them - and when this is come 'they' shall step forth as fellow beings- and as one prepared for to give unto thee a hand in love- and with joy--

They ask no other reward other than to be accepted for that which they are- and that ye be prepared for thy new part of the great and divine plan- such is wisdom to prepare thyself- for it is neigh time when there shall be no more time--

I say time is swiftly running out- and ye shall find thyself outside- and wherein there is no comfort- and sad shall they be which are found wanting- so be it and Selah.

Blest are they which seek out them which are sent- it is not given unto thee to know 'them' until ye have prepared thyself- then they shall reveal themselves unto thee---

I say they shall find thee - be ye assured of that- for they are alert- and there is no hiding place- it is by thy light that they find thee--they go not into the den of the porcupine-

They go not into the dragons den---

I say ye shall be found when ye have prepared thyself- Blest shall ye be so be it and Selah.

I come that ye may be prepared- so be about thy preparation- I shall wait thy call. I am the older brother and thy Sibor- Soran.

Recorded by Sister Thedra of the Emerald Cross

Beloved of my being:- Be ye blest of me this day- and ye shall be blest- so be it and Selah.

I come this day that they may have this my word - and PRAISE ye the Father Mother God from whom ALL came- and to which ye shall return---

Bless them which reach out - that ye may be spared the torment which shall be experienced by the traitors--

I say they shall experience great/ and much torment--long shall they wander in darkness--for it is now come when the gates shall be closed --

And I say the call has gone out- and we have said over and over again 'be ye as ones prepared to enter therein...' and they stand with feet of lead--their hearts hardened- and their fingers in their ears---

I say unto them - THEY SHALL HEAR! -- yet it may be another age-- when they have experienced much sorrow-- yet it is better late than never--

So we WAIT- for the day when we might assist them--and blest shall they be when they do turn their face homeward---

I say unto <u>them</u> which do wait - that they shall be as the ones which betray themself- and they shall cry out in their suffering- and in their misery for help- and it shall not come--for we thy Sibors do work unto the season- we are sent at this time of God the Father for this season- this harvest---

And them which are not ready are as ones which refuse to awaken- for we are crying from every land upon the earth--

We stand waiting thy call- we are prepared for any call- any emergency- and we are not traitors unto ourselves - neither do we betray the ones who give unto us their trust and credit for being that which we are---

I say when they do ask of God the Father their freedom- and place within HIM their faith He shall send one of HIS SONS unto them - yea, He shall send a legion of his hosts- and He is ALMIGHTY - ALL WISE--

None shall take from HIM HIS power --

He is glad this day is come- when the BRIDGE is formed-

I say it is a two way BRIDGE- and we come and go- and we bring thee which are prepared- and we return thee when ye have learned well thy lessons---

And let it be recorded herein that many do come as thy LORD and MASTER Jesus/Sananda- known as the CHRIST-JESUS- even as He- resurrected from thy so-called dead---

I say many things are accomplished while ye walk about in thy sleep- ye are in darkness and know not that which goes on about thee---

I say ye shall be alert and about thy preparation and ye shall be as one illumined---

I say great revelation shall be given unto thee so be it I have spoken for this day- let it be for the good of all mankind---

Blest are the hands which serve me---

I am thy brother and thy Sibor--Sori Sori.

Recorded by Sister Thedra of the Emerald Cross

Beloved ones - seeking to walk in the light of service and love to all life- thou art needed- greatly needed- and the time grows short--

Ye are not as yet prepared to take thy part- ye are being prepared to take thy part as fast as thy life-streams will permit-- ye cannot be processed beyond thy capacity to assimilate that which is given---

The minds of all who serve must be pliant-- all opinions must be freed from thy consciousness-- ye must know- and KNOW that ye KNOW the TRUTH only!

Be patient yet a little while- soon ye will know the glory ye had before the world was--- Ye walked with thy Father Mother God and knew no suffering- ye will again-- and all thy suffering will be forgotten---

Be ye mindful of thy inheritance and ask of thy Sibors for all that ye need to assist ye in gaining thy goal---

Lo I am with thee always-- ye are never alone-- thy silent watchers are mindful of thee-- but ye must ask- it is the Law.

I am thy Sibor and Brother Sananda.

Recorded by Sorea Sorea

THE SUPREME TEST

Blest of my being:- Blest art thou this day- and blest shall ye be- I am with thee that ye may be blest- forever blest.

Be ye as my hand made manifest unto them- and say unto them in my name- that - Ye shall be as one on whose shoulders rest great responsibility- for therein is the supreme test of thy loyalty and of thy greatness!

I say when it is come that the days of trial shall overtake thee shall ye endure-- or shall ye faint and perish?

I say be ye now prepared for the time which shall come-- I say ye shall go out from the place of thy abode- and ye shall go into the place which is new and strange - and ye shall walk upright as human being---

And for them which are prepared - it shall be a place of great beauty and light- for each shall be in his own environment- which he has created for himself---

I say ye shall begin this day to create it-- and ye shall be alert and give unto me credit for knowing that which I say unto thee- for I have the greater vision- and I am free to read the records---

I say ye shall be removed from the earth into a new place wherein are the ones like unto thyself in development- and ye do not escape thy environment---

I say ye are thy own preparation- and responsible for thy own deliverance from bondage-- ye shall choose this day which ye shall serve--darkness or light---

Be ye wise in thy decision---

I am now prepared to assist thee - yet the preparation is thine!

I point the way- ye walk in it--

And ye shall blame NO OTHER for thy failure to obey the law.

Nor shall ye give another credit for saving thee--for there IS NO VICARIOUS ATONEMENTS within the realm of being -- IT DOES NOT EXIST---

Ye are the one to atone for all thy misused energy- and ye are the one which shall correct all thy errors-- and err no more---

So be it that thy Sibors stand ready to assist thee in thy efforts- when ye have done thy best-- we shall lend thee a hand in brotherly love and with wisdom which is endowed unto us of God the Father.

I am with thee by day and by night - yet I stand with hands tied until ye ask assistance of God the Father which has given unto thee being- and then by law- I am freed to give unto thee as ye are prepared to receive--NO MORE-- NO LESS---

I am not a poor SON OF GOD--- ALL HE HAS IS MINE to give - and when ye are prepared I shall give unto thee as He has given unto me---

I am the Wayshower- and I come to point the way--walk ye in it and blest shall ye be---

I am Sananda Son of the ALMIGHTY ADORABLE ALLWISE FATHER MOTHER so be it and Selah.

Recorded by Sister Thedra of the Emerald Cross

NEVER AGAIN---

Beloved of my being be ye blest of me and by me-- I am come that ye may be blest--- And now I speak unto thee that they might have light so be it that they which have eyes to see and ears to hear- and a receptive heart shall see and hear - and receive these my words unto themself - and they shall be blest---

Know ye this -- In as much as ye receive my words- ye receive me --I say ye which do not receive my words shall not see me---

Never again- shall ye put thy fingers into my wounded side-- NEVER! - it is finished--ye do not keep open my wounds- it is finished-- it is finished---

Ye which do demand proof shall go on in thy delerium- and thy own wonton ways-- ye shall NOT go into the dens of the porcupine demanding proof of me---

I say ye shall be confounded and confused-- ye find me not in thy edifices of stone- which ye have set up- and named for thyself.

Ye have taken it upon thyself to build them of stone and mortar- glass- marble- metal- and all other available material -- ye have gone the long way to find me -- yet ye close me out- I say ye close me out--and it is so!

I speak! And I know that which I say to be true-- Ye celebrate thy season of resurrection with a display of thy raiment--- Ye go into the places of worship- so called- for thy own gratification of pride!

Ye are unto thyself traitor- ye are hypocrites-- and I know that which ye are. Ye are not an enigma unto me for I see thy record--I watch thee--

Thy heart is troubled- and ye are filled with fear and misgivings- ye point a finger at my servants- ye betray thy own self--

Wherein is it said - Ye are not of the light--- Ye are used to the dark and therein ye are blind- ye see not in the light--- until thine eyes are accustomed unto it---

I have said unto thee - when ye are so prepared I shall give unto thee a portion- and it shall be unto thee all things- and ye shall be free of all bondage forever---

I have spoken-- and I am a Son of God- born of God eternally free- and I say that which should profit thee- ye have but to accept it in the name of the Father Mother God- so be it my part to speak unto thee as HE would have me-I am thy older brother- the Wayshower--- Sananda-

Beloved of my being - be ye as my hand made manifest unto them- And say unto them as I would say that - MIGHTY IS THE LAW- and GREAT, GREAT is the POWER thereof -- and SWIFT is the RETRIBITION THEREOF--- I say it is now come when there shall be GREAT and mighty repercussion from and by/through the law which has been set into motion by the MISUSE of the energy which is sent forth/ in, through and by these scripts---

Now it is given unto me to give these words unto thee that they may come to know that the law is NO RESPECTOR OF PERSONS-- and it is SWIFT in its ACTION--

When the POWER is used to gratify the <u>selfish ego of man</u>- to prove their opinions and their plan- to be unto them their stay and their staff on which to build up <u>their theories</u> and OPINIONS WOE unto them--

Words are inadequate to describe the law- yet I say unto them which are taking away and adding to-- that it shall be given unto me to see and to know that which they do/ have done/ and shall do---

I say they shall be cut off-- Yea- cast out into utter darkness-- Now ye shall give these words unto them- and they shall go out before the date allotted unto them- for it is my part to speak unto them that they be warned- and spared- much torment- for they are their own tormentors-- and I say they shall save themself - from themself----

They shall be held accountable for that which they do- and when any indiscretion/ any comment which is unlike LOVE- and like unto blasphemy is directed unto the GODHEAD it is not within my POWER by law to prevent the results - which is swift indeed---

I say again the retribution is swift indeed--- So be it that ye shall be as one responsible for every word which proceeds out of thy mouth-- ye shall be as one prepared to receive that which returns unto thee a thousand fold- from that which ye have sent out upon the earth- I say it picks up its kind and returns unto thee ONE THOUSAND FOLD!

And no man woman or creature can prevent it-- be ye what ye create for thyself---

I come that ye may have light- so be ye blest of me and by me I am thy Sibor and thy Brother.

Sananda.

Recorded by Sister Thedra

Beloved of my being- I greet thee this hour with my hand upon thy head- and I stand as one alert unto thy part- and I say unto thee: ye are as my hand made manifest unto them in the world of men---

I say ye shall give unto them this word- and it shall profit them to heed it- for it is my part given unto me of the Father Mother God for thee/for them-- And I say they are now in the last days of OLD CYCLE- going into the New-- Yea even into the NEW by many, many days! Yea years in thy way of calculating time---

I say ye have come into the NEW-- yet some sleep- as there was nothing else---

I say it is the way of the dragon to give unto them portions to beguile them- that their sleep be not ended-- yet they sleep a troubled sleep- and they are in lethargy---

While we of the higher realm CRY - AWAKEN! ALL YE CHILDREN OF THE LAND AWAKEN---

So be it that our LOVE exceeds our PATIENCE- for thy time endeth. While our LOVE is everlasting- so be it and Selah---

I say ye shall AWAKEN! And ye know not the hour- nor the place for ye shall go into deep sleep- and therein is the pity -- so be it we give unto thee of our love - our energy - our wisdom that ye may be spared!

So be it that ye shall accept us for that which we are- and ye shall ask for LIGHT- and yet ye shall follow the laws set down for thee.-

I say again- we do not sibor fools- nor do we give unto babes the priceless jewels who know not their worth---

I am now within the earth as man- manifested as man--

I walk with feet as man--

I speak as man-- and I am prepared to come unto thee as ye are prepared to receive me---

Yet ye shall be as one free from all thy conceit-- all thy hypocrisy-- all thy pre conceived ideas of me---

I am not thy POOR BLOODY PRIEST!

I AM THE SON OF GOD THE FATHER--the one sent of GOD the Father that ye may be delivered up---

Praise His holy name - and give unto Him thanks in <u>all things</u> for he is mindful of thee - and he has sent me forth that ye might find thy way home-- so be it a glad day when ye return unto him---

I speak with thee that ye may turn thy face homeward- so be it and Selah.

I am Sananda Son of God---

Beloved of my being-- Upon this ground shall ye stand and declare for them their freedom- and ye shall be as one in authority- for I say it is so- SO BE IT--and none shall deny thee---

So be it that I am he which is sent to do the will of the Father-- and it is by HIS WILL that I have ordained thee in the PRIESTHOOD of MELCHEZEDEC---

I say that ye are as one ordained of GOD the FATHER---

That ye have been given the authority and the power to go out among them and to speak the words which HE shall put into thy mouth---And HE shall speak and it shall become.

I say unto thee HE shall speak and it shall be done- so let it be.

I say it is true- so be it- and no man shall make void my word---

I speak with the power and authority given unto me of HIM the Father Mother God---

I bless thee my sister of the EMERALD CROSS---

I now command thee to give them this document- and it shall go on record as my authority of GOD THE FATHER- and I give unto thee as he gives unto me- such is my divine right-- I say it is so be it and be it so and SELAH.

Ye shall henceforth from this day forth walk in my foot steps and ye shall be as my hand- and my foot upon the earth-- and I shall be with thee unto the end---

I am thy Sibor and thy older Brother---

Sananda-

Recorded by Sister Thedra

Blest art thou Oh My child-- Be ye as my hand made manifest unto them this day- and say unto them in my name that- I AM the Father Mother Eternal which has given unto them being and they which I have sent forth of My Being---.

And ye shall be as My hands and My feet upon the earth- as My voice- and as My eyes- ye shall see Me in all thy day-- ye shall see by night---.

Ye shall counsel with Me--

Ye shall look within for thy being- and NOT afar---

I say ye are Me- and I AM thee-- there is NO SEPARATION- ONLY within thy THINKING!

I say ye think and it is so- ye will it that ye return unto Me and it is done---

I speak unto thee that ye may come to know Me- and were it not so ye could NOT BE-- ye speak forth that which I WILL and ye receive it-- and ' THINK ' it into thy image and it becomes that which ye image---

Ye do not keep My commandment and "KEEP THE WORD HOLY" I say ye have adulterated My word- for it goes out into manifestation perfect- ye receive it- and ye condition it into thy IMAGE- BECAUSE OF THY OWN THINKING---

Ye are as yet not of MY MIND- for ye have closed thyself off from Me-- I say once in time which is no more- ye were one with Me- ye counseled with Me- ye have forgotten thy inheritance---

And ye have now been given a NEW DISPENSATION whereby ye shall walk with Me this day---

The gate has been opened- and the bridge has been finished-- and I say unto thee there are many returning unto Me this day- and ye know it not- for ye are asleep!

I say unto the ones which are prepared- YE SHALL THIS DAY ARISE AS ON WINGS OF LIGHT AND ASCEND UNTO ME- EVEN AS MY ROYAL SONS---

I say- I say there are ones among thee whom I have sent- that are now prepared to give unto thee the waters of life- and too I say the Water of Life is a tangible substance- made visible by My touch- from and of Me--

It is My SPOKEN WORD MADE SUBSTANCE- and appears unto thee as liquid light- and therein lies thy salvation---

I say unto thee in the WATER OF LIFE LIES THE SUBSTANCE OF CREATION-- 'ALL THAT IS PERFECT'- So be it that ye shall drink this substance and it shall free thee from all dense form-- all Earth gravity- all attraction of the Moon-- ye shall arise as one eternally free-- Ye shall become a LIVING SUBSTANCE- AS LIGHT MADE FLESH-- AS THE LIGHT OF THE WORLD---

Ye shall be as My heart beat- as My pulse- ye shall hear My voice- ye shall see me face to face- and none other shall deny My words for I speak unto thee as thy ETERNAL FATHER MOTHER GOD/CAUSE OF THY BEING---.

And because thou hast turned unto me I speak unto thee-- and because thou hast asked for the good of all mankind I have accepted thee and I am glad this day that thou hast chosen to return unto me of thy own free will---

For long thou hast gone from me-- So long have ye wandered in darkness which has held thee from me---

My longing is great-- My heart shall be filled when ALL MY CHILDREN return unto me-- And I shall receive them with gladness and there shall be great rejoicing throughout MY KINGDOM---

I AM thy hand -

I AM thy voice -

I AM thy breath -

I AM thy mind---

GLORIFY me- and

I shall receive thee unto myself ---

I AM THY FATHER MOTHER GOD---

Solen Solen Aum Solen

Recorded by Sister Thedra

THE ETERNAL MOTHER SPEAKS OF LOVE

Beloved of my being--

Blest be this day--

Blest art thou Oh my child--

Be ye as my hand made manifest unto them--

Praise ye Oh my soul--

Praise thee Oh my child--

Praise unto the Father Mother God--

Praise ye Him for evermore- sing

Praise unto Him- let thy heart rejoice and be glad---

I am come that it may be so- so let it be---

I am thy Mother Eternal--

I am Sarah the Mother of Abraham--

I am thy Mother God--

I am His part which is LOVE--

I send thee forth in love- and with my hand

I write that which is written--

I speak what is spoken through thy lips--

I speak and it is prompted in love- therefore

I do not speak -- for

I am LOVE---

I say that which is good for all mankind---

I bless them by the spoken word--

I give unto them that which they can comprehend---

I speak unto them while they sleep- and

I cause them to hear me- yet they arise from their beds and

go their way forgetting that which

I have said- yet they shall be caused to remember it---

and not one word shall be lost- for when it has gone out

it returns bringing back its fruits- and with great

abundance -such is the law-

I speak unto thee of LOVE which

I am--

I am the MOTHER- and

I give unto thee my love and

I cause thy heart to over flow with love- and the joy of

Mothering them- yet ye shall not deprive them of their

Lessons---a lesson learned is a lesson earned- so let

it be---

I give unto thee of myself that ye may walk gently-

and with dignity--be ye glad for this day and

I shall touch thee and

I shall cause thy cup to spill over- so let it be--

Sarah.

Recorded by Sister Thedra of the Emerald Cross

Behold me - I come unto thee in my holy Christ body-- I stand before thee as man- made flesh-- I say I come as man made flesh. I sit before thee as man - yet ye see not my HOLY CHRIST BODY which speaks unto thee-- While my body of flesh remains silent before thee---

I say unto thee I am with thee in flesh and in SPIRIT-- I speak unto thee in SPIRIT -- and of SPIRIT -- and in Spirit do ye receive me- such is SPIRIT--- And the way of SPIRIT is beyond MAN'S comprehension---

Yet he shall comprehend all things through SPIRIT REVELATION---

I say that revelation is a gift of GOD THE FATHER--- Now I speak unto thee as thy brother Joel of Arcadia- yet ye see me-- and ye see me not-- as man ye see me-- as Spirit I do dwell within man-- Yet I am free as SPIRIT- and as Spirit I am not bound-- so be it I am bound as <u>flesh</u> - yet flesh shall be redeemed and transmuted forever free from bondage---

Now I say unto thee it is come when even the atoms of our bodies shall be transmuted and set free- AND THIS WILL BE THE DAY- so be it and Selah--

I am Joel of Arcadia.

Received through the HOLY CHRIST SPIRIT and recorded by Sister Thedra.

"HE IS COME"

Be ye this day twice blest- for I come unto thee as thy brother from out the Temple of Light-- I speak unto thee upon a subject dear unto My heart- I say unto thee one has come into thy midst unknown unto the sleepers--.

And He walks gently- OH SO GENTLY!

Yet He is all POWERFULL- ALL - WISE- and is LOVE personalized- and He has within His hand the power and the authority to create worlds- yea to people them--.

I say HE it is which walks among thee- and He has gone the long way to bring thee home--.

I am not a far off- nor am I in darkness- nor bondage-- I speak unto thee as a free man- free born of God the Father- I have drunken of the water of Life and I am eternally free- forever free--.

I speak with thee that they might have these my words- for thou hast prepared thyself for to receive Me- and for this I am glad for not all are so prepared---

Now ye shall say unto them in My name- that one which has come into their midst walketh among them- as one of them-- and as one which has the AUTHORITY and the POWER to give unto them the WATER of LIFE---.

Yet they shall be as one prepared to receive it- and none shall deceive HIM-- and be ye not a traitor unto thyself-- every thought- and ye shall watch thy words- thy motives-- for I say unto thee ye are the reflection of that which is in thy heart- So be it and SELAH.

I speak unto thee as one which sees and knows thee-- I am not a fool- nor am I from the NETHERWORLD- I speak as the Father would have Me speak- and I am not separated from Him.

Now within a short while the ONE which I speak of shall go out into thy midst as man- He shall seek out the ones which are prepared- and He shall find them one by one and He shall give unto them that which shall prepare them for their work which is to be done in the time which is coming soon-- coming sure as the dawn draweth nigh--

He shall walk with surety of purpose and with LOVE- He shall be firm in all His dealings- He shall make no allowances for color- or parts. He shall not frown upon the infirmed- and the unlearned- He shall give unto them as they are prepared to receive--

He shall be glad for HIS PART- and unto it He shall be true-- justice shall be within Him- He shall be as one upon whose head the Sun never sets- He shall walk with feet of LIGHT- He shall touch them and they shall be changed in the twinkling of an eye—

I speak wisely for I know HIM- I walk with HIM- I am his brother- His COMPANION-

I am too a FREE BORN MAN OF GOD--

I wait for the next visit- I then shall speak of another which is to come- yet this ONE shall go out before HIM ---

Be ye not deceived- and find thyself cut off- or found wanting- Be ye not as the foolish Virgins---

I speak as a brother in LOVE and COMPASSION.

I Am thy older Brother   Soran.

Recorded by Sister Thedra

THE TREADMILL OF REINCARNATION
SANANDA

Beloved-- I speak unto thee this day that THEY may know me and that which I say unto thee-they shall bear witness of these my words-- and ye shall give them unto the ones which are so prepared to receive them-- and blest shall they be---

Ye shall say unto them as I would - that in the days just ahead that many shall go into their new places of abode as ones prepared for them-- and there shall be not one out of his environment---

Yet I say unto them it behooves them to improve their environment, for it is come when they shall awaken to find themself bound within yet another place-- in an environment not unlike their present one---

And they shall find themself bound still unto the tread-mill of reincarnation-- and therein is the pity!

For a NEW DISPENSATION has been given unto thee that ye might be free from this law--I say that ye might be free from the law of incarnation- so let it be finished this day---

I come that ye might be free-- and yet ye have not been unto me a disciple- and ye have not given unto me thy hand---

I stand with mine outstretched- and with my open arms extended- and yet ye turn thy face from me-- ye have but to open up thine arms- thy heart- and invite me in and I shall come in and abide with thee- so let it profit thee---

And ye shall be as a disciple-- ye shall 'DISCIPLINE' thyself -- and be mindful of me- and that which I say unto thee-- and ye shall abide by the laws set down for thee for they are sufficient unto thee-- And I shall come in and Sibor thee in the "GREATER PART" ---

Now let it be said that - "There are none so foolish as the one which thinks himself wise-- and none so sad as the one which betrays themself."

I say again- there are none so foolish- as the fools-- and none so sad as the traitors- they are the saddest of the lot- so be it and SELAH. Pity are they for they shall wait a long while ere they are given a NEW DISPENSATION- for the gate shall be closed- and they shall find themself outside and they shall begin from the beginning- so be it and SELAH.

I speak unto thee that ye might alert thyself -- and forget not that I am watchful of thee-- and I do not say ye are hopeless- I SAY- YE ARE IN LETHARGY- AND ASLEEP---

and I stand ready to come unto thee at they call- yet ye shall respond unto me in this day- and it is most foolish to wait-- for there is NO TOMORROW!

And YESTERDAY is NOT- and there is only THIS DAY-which ye have- and that is not thine to hold- nor to give---

I say ye shall arise and alert thyself and be at Peace and seek the LIGHT which is eternal- without end---

I am thy Brother and thy Sibor- Sananda.

* * *

Beloved of my being - be ye as my hand made manifest unto them this day- and say unto them as I would say- that this is MY DAY WHICH I HAVE CHOSEN FOR MY PART- wherein I have come unto thee for the purpose of giving unto thee that which the FATHER MOTHER GOD has WILLED unto thee---

I say the Father has sent me at this time that ye may be brought in- ye have waited long for this day-- ye have gone in and out of the bodies of flesh as so many garments- shodilly made and discarded as such---

Ye have slept for a time and stirred thyself and rushed back into the world of manifested flesh as so many unknowing ones-- forgetting that which ye have learned in thy former garments of flesh.

I say thy memory is blanked from thee-- and it is now come when ye may have thy memory restored unto thee- which is the Fathers WILL- so be it I shall be glad to do my part that this may be accomplished---

I am now prepared to give unto thee a part which shall be unto thee thy memory- I have the authority and the right to give unto thee a portion which shall be unto thee thy freedom from bondage- such is my word unto thee so be it and Selah---

I ask of thee- PONDER THESE MY WORDS- AND IT SHALL PROFIT THEE---I am thy Sibor and thy Older Brother--- Sananda-

Recorded by Sister Thedra

Channeled thru Sister Sorea Sorea--

Many walk in darkness not knowing their blindness and nothing will change them- they rush toward destruction and naught can stay their headlong plunge--- This ye see on every side- waste not thy time on those who will not be staid-- rather give thy time to those who are of a mind to learn---

Thou are my hands made manifest unto these- they shall have their reward-- twice blest are they-- You too are in darkness for yet a little time but thy day will dawn in a blaze of light so bright ye will be dazzled- thou are led as the blind now, but soon ye shall walk with certainty and knowing- this I promise thee.

I am thy Elder Brother -Sananda.

MANY ARE ASCENDING

Beloved of my being - Be ye as my hand made manifest unto them this day- and say unto them that which I shall give unto thee to say- and it shall profit them- for it is now come when there shall be great and many changes upon the earth---

I say that there shall be many which go into their new places of abode which are unprepared for the change- and they shall be as ones confused- and they shall be as ones which have gone the long way-- for they have not prepared themself for this way.

And it is now come when many are being translated- and which are ascending unto their new places- free from all the earths endearments--all the gravitation of the earth- all the attraction of the moon - and the elements there of -- they are free from all bondage ---

I say unto the sleepers- they have been given a NEW Dispensation - a NEW DAY/a NEW LAW-- and they shall stir themself and ARISE-- and turn homeward--

I say they which do shall be brought in-- I am come that they might be--- Such is my part- and such is the will of the Father--

Has HE not commanded thee-- "GO FIND MY SHEEP?"

Have ye not gone out?

Have I not put within thy hands the food? When they accept it blest shall they be-- yet when they reject it - PITY are they!

I say I have called many- for many are given into my keeping and I shall not rest until I have delivered them out of bondage- yet they shall come of their own free will - blest shall they be---

I say this day that I stand helpless before them which close me out-- I simply wait--yet they shall find the waiting hard to bear- they shall be tormented of their own longing- and of their own way-- and when there is no other way they shall turn unto the source of their being- such is the law---

I say they shall turn unto their source in the last day so be it and SELAH--

I am with thee that ye may be prepared - and that ye may be my hand and my foot upon the earth-- for I am within the earth as man - and many hands have I - many servants have I- and I shall remember them in the day of stress - such is my nature/my love for them---

I am thy older Brother and thy Sibor, Sananda.

Recorded by Sister Thedra

BEREA (VENUS) SPEAKS

Berea speaking-- unto thee MY CHILD--that ye may be as my hands made manifest unto them---

I say unto them - that wherein I am there is no sorrow other than thy wonton thy suffering--thou art our sorrow! Yet ye walk about as ROBOTS-animated by that which ye know not.

I say ye shall be as ones quickened - and ye shall come alive-- Ye shall be as ones willing to hear the voice of thy Eternal Parent.

Ye shall be as ones tormented of thy own longing and of thy own way until ye turn unto Him the SOURCE of thy being- and seek of HIM the LIGHT- which is His to give. Ye shall be as ones cut off until ye turn unto Him and ask for thy freedom- so be it and SELAH.

I say unto thee blest are they which turn unto HIM-- I say we here in this temple know the joy of serving HIM by day and by night--for we do not sleep- we are alert and refreshed from His own hand-- we are not cut off as thou art/we have not cut ourselves off as thou hast---

I speak unto thee as one which knows thee- and thy way-- thy longings have been great- thy suffering pitiful-- Yet ye have not turned homeward as SONS of GOD-- Ye are loth to obey the laws set before thee- ye are loth to be a disciple of the SON- Sent of HIM that ye too may follow him the SON of GOD sent so long ago---

And again and again has he come - yet ye have not been unto thyself true- ye have gone the long way round-- ye have chosen thy way-- and none other shall bear the responsibility of thy salvation.

Yet ye shall be as ones responsive unto us thy Sibors which stand ready and OH SO WILLING to help thee- our Love is INFINITE-- our strength is of Him the Father-- our authority is given of HIM -- Yet our patience is weakened-- and our time is short- for there is much to do and so little time---

I say so little time-- for everything is done according unto the law-- Now I say unto thee the time draws near when ye shall be removed from the earth- and ye shall be as ones responsible for thy own place of abode- for thy own welfare---

Beloved Ones I stand upon the threshold of this temple of LOVE wherein I abide-- I speak unto thee from the depth of my being and I speak as one which knows—

I say that in the time which is near that ye shall be removed from thy place of abode into yet another and ye shall be as one responsible for thy own place wherein ye shall be put---

Ye shall hear me-- and be ye prepared for thy own place wherein ye shall go-- I say not all places are as thine where in ye are- not all as mine wherein I am---

I say there are many dwelling places within the solar system- galaxies without end---

I say we are free/and not bound unto any one of them- yet we should not be content to be bound within any one of them-- for we know what "FREEDOM" means! While ye do not---

We see thee as a sad lot- as the little ones in darkness- stumbling in darkness- when there is light abundantly--- Ye need not wait--- The day is at hand---

I say the day is now come when ye shall walk and talk with the SONS of GOD- the SONS of the ETERNAL LIGHT-- they know the Father to be the Source of their BEING-- they know the Mother to be the LOVE which SUSTAINS them-- they know the SONS to be THEMSELF-- they are not divided against the ETERNAL PARENT- neither against themself ---

They each have a part within the divine plan- and none trespass upon the past of the other -- and they are as ones without any quarrel or criticism one for the other---

I say they are <u>ONE</u> - and they KNOW that which is the <u>truth</u> which shall set thee free---

I say that within this shall ye be free from all animosity-- all hatred- all war- all transgression-

I say when ye come to LOVE thy GOD thy FATHER MOTHER- ye shall LOVE ALL THINGS which HE has endowed unto thee as CREATION of HIS HAND- as the CREATION of HIS BREATH- breathed out of HIS mouth/made manifest in the world of the seen---

Ye shall be as ones prepared for the "GREATER PART." For ONE shall walk among thee as HIS HANDS and as HIS FEET-- And in as much as ye prepare thyself HE shall come unto thee - and He shall touch thee and ye shall be quickened and ye shall know HIM---

And He shall give unto thee a portion which shall serve thee well-- Ye shall be as one free from the gravitation of the earth- and free from the attraction of the moon--ye shall have the law of the elements revealed unto thee-- ye shall be forever free from all bondage---

Ye shall be free to go and come at will into any galaxy-- ye shall be ONE with the law of being-- ye shall wear upon thy head the crown of the SUN -- ye shall walk as a SON-- ye shall know thyself to be a SON of GOD the Father---

And it is again recorded within these scripts of the SIBORS PORTIONS-- and ye have but to ask for them-- yet ye shall take the necessary steps to support- to promulgate the work---

I say this is the teaching of the Saints- the "SAVIORS" of them which have been directed in the INNER WAY--

I say these are the teachings of the MASTERS which ye have so vainly sought--

I say ye have sought in vain- and for thy own end-- ye have no need to seek further--for ye shall prepare thyself and the ONE ye would call "MASTER" shall come unto thee- and all thy waiting shall end- so be it and SELAH---

I speak unto thee thusly-- for there is a great need for standing within thy realm---

I say - PONDER THESE MY WORDS- give unto me credit for knowing that which I say and I shall be mindful of thee in the days of struggle and trials---

I shall speak unto thee and ye shall listen for my voice---

Cut out the inharmony of man-- close it out-- let LOVE reign supreme-- let JOY be within thee---

Bless them which misuse thee---

Be unto them a lamp unto their feet---

I say ye shall be unto them a lamp-- and I shall give unto thee as the Father would have me---

I am thy older SISTER and thy Sibor- known as Venus-- I am the complement of our Beloved Sanat Kumara- Beloved of GOD-- Bless Him for his part- for he is one of thy beloved Benefactors-

Berea... (Venus)

Recorded by Sister Thedra

Beloved Ones whom I have brought unto this altar—

Be ye blest this day and I say unto thee it is now come when mighty shall be thy power and thy light-- ye shall be as my light-- as my voice-- as my hand- my feet- for I shall direct thee in thy ways.

I shall speak and ye shall hear - and ye shall respond unto me-- I shall bless thee by day and by night---

I shall call unto thee and ye shall hear me- and ye shall rejoice that it is come- when we shall walk and talk together-- I shall direct thee in all thy ways-

I shall give unto thee a part separate from all others--

I shall give unto thee the part which I have saved for thee--

I shall give unto thee as I have received--

I shall do all these things and more--

I shall bring thee into the place wherein I am and instruct thee in the ways which I know--

I shall be unto thee Sibor- and I shall give unto thee that for which ye have waited- so be ye as one prepared for to receive it-- Thy waiting shall end- so let it be now- and I shall be glad--

Go thy way in peace- I shall speak with thee again this day and be ye as one prepared to receive me-- I am Sananda --

Recorded by Sister Thedra---

Received and recorded by Sorea Sorea:

The part of thy Sibors is to instruct - it is yours to learn- ye are here for that purpose-- open thy minds and hearts to all that is given thee -- be diligent in thy practice of this work which is given thee. We do no idle thing- not speak idle words--- We are serious- and this is serious work---

Ye shall be helped in all ye do if ye but respond to that which is given thee--- We who work on this side of life are not able to do your work- ye must do all that is asked of thee- that this work shall be done in accordance with the plan---

This is serious times- and it is the greater part of wisdom that ye be alert and obedient--- We ask of the obedience above all-ye must be obedient and do the work-- ye are not to neglect the calls that are given ye will be blest according to thy effort and answer to the voice of thy Sibors---

We are awaiting thy cooperation- <u>be ye alert</u>- and ye shall have thy reward --- I am thy Brother Bor--

Recorded by Sorea Sorea

THE WATER OF LIFE

Beloved of my being be ye as my hand made manifest unto them- and say unto them as I would say- that there are many among them which would deliver them out of bondage- should they prepare themself for to receive them---

Now it is come when much shall be accomplished within a short while-- and within that time one shall come into the place where ye are- and he shall walk with thee and he shall talk with thee as man---And he shall be as my hand made manifest unto thee- and he as one in authority - and he shall have the power for that which shall be given unto him to do-- he shall be as one prepared for his part---

Now in the time left for this part- he shall find many which shall drink of the water of LIFE- and he shall be as one qualified to give unto them- as they are so prepared

Blest shall they be - be ye one among them---

I speak of the water of LIFE again-- for as yet ye know not of this substance---

I say it is the substance of LIFE- from which cometh all things perfect-- from which all things perfect are created-- I say ye know NOT this substance for ye have NOT had the purity of heart to use it- ye have not had the MIND to use it---

For it is "THE PEARL WITHOUT PRICE"

I say it is the LIFE substance which renews and sustains all particles of life--yet ye only condition it-- ye do not create anything which is perfect---

I say ye are CREATORS in thy own right-ye create like unto the WHORE--- I say ye create with thy 'mind' like unto the own O not with the MIND of the _ ONE GOD- Father Mother- like unto them perfect---

I say they are ONE _ 'perfection' in all that which they create from the liquid substance ---

I say it is the WORD of GOD made manifest--- And all which do drink of this substance shall become perfect in HIM of HIM and by HIM and for HIS sake---

I speak unto thee again for thy sake- that ye may bear in mind that ye are not without hope-- without aid-- I say we come that ye may know and know that ye KNOW-- and blest shall ye be---

Be ye blest of me- I am the Wayshower--

I go before thee—Sananda-

Recorded- by Sister Thedra

Beloved of my being--Behold me- I say behold me-- I stand before thee- ye see me not as man- yet ye know I am with thee---

I come that ye may know-- I say that ye may know---

I come that ye may be blest---

I say unto thee be ye as one which has my hand upon thee- and I say unto thee I am with them which I brought- and which I sent back unto their respective places of abode--and I give unto each a different part---

Yet they shall work as 'one' - they shall be as ONE in SPIRIT—

And they shall be as ONE in HEART - they shall walk side by side knowing themself to be SISTERS -- and they shall not go against the law-- they shall not be divided against each other-- or against themself-- they shall be of ONE MIND--- They shall be mindful of the LAW set down ---they shall be of a mind to learn and they shall not deny that which is said unto them--- They shall listen for my words- and they shall hear -- so be it and Selah.

I come unto thee that they may be blest this day-- they go their way in peace-- I am the PORTER at the gate--and I shall see that no harm befalls them---

Be ye blest - for I shall be unto thee both food and drink--I shall be unto the raiment- and LIGHT--I shall be warmth and comfort-- Yea- I shall be unto thee all things which so ever ye ask---

I give unto thee MY SEPTER- MY ORB--

I am prepared for this part--so be it that ye have prepared thyself for to receive me--and as ye are prepared so I come - I come - I come-- blest be this day-- I am Sananda- Son of God--- Recorded by Sister Thedra.

Sanat Kumara Speaking-

Beloved of My being- be ye blest of Me and by Me- for it is come when this day shall bear fruit- and ye shall be as one blest of Me for I shall I give unto thee a part which shall be for the good of all mankind- and ye shall be unto them My hand made manifest--

I say I shall give unto thee a part which shall be for the good of all mankind and ye shall give it unto them--for it is now come when great shall be their need- so be it that I am come that they may be helped - I give unto them as the Father would have Me- so be it and Selah---

Blest shall they be- I say they shall be blest---

with this shall ye go unto them- and ye shall need no other authority- for it is the sign and the insignia which they shall come to recognize- I say it is my seal which I give unto thee-- so be it the seal I am given of the Father for thee---

I come unto thee that ye may receive of HIM- for I am sent- even as - Sananda our beloved benefactor- that ye may receive of the Father- so be it and SELAH. Be ye unto them that which I am unto thee- and ye shall be as one in authority- for have I not given unto thee my word of command- I speak unto thee as the Father has commanded Me--

I now command thee in HIS name go forth- commanding of them obedience unto the law- and say unto them in the name of the Father Son that they shall walk in the way set before them- I say they shall turn neither to the left nor to the right- for I am not of a mind to sibor fools- for they are the laggards- which are of a mind to sleep and they will have their day—

This is the day of the LORD- when they shall alert themself and come forth as the Sons of God- they shall be their own saviors- they shall have no false gods- they shall be obedient unto the law set down within these scripts-- I say these are not the only scripts-- yet these laws cover all that is written- or shall be- and I say blest shall they be which are prepared in the day of the coming of the KING- for mighty shall be HIS word and exacting the law---

Be ye as one prepared---

I Am thy brother and thy Sibor--

Sanat Kumara

Recorded by Sister Thedra

Beloved- I come unto thee at this time for the purpose of saying that which is given unto Me of the Father Mother God--

I bless thee this day with these words-- "SOLEN AUM SOLEN" I say BLEST BE THE NAME OF SOLEN--- Glad shall ye be for this day--

I come unto thee that ye be blest- for this do I come-- Great and MIGHTY is the word SOLEN AUM SOLEN--

Praise His Holy name-- Give unto Him praise and thanks---

I say unto thee-- ALL THE GLORY IS HIS---

Be ye as one prepared for the greater part---

I say unto thee-- Praise the Father Mother God- unto HIM all the PRAISE and the GLORY---

I am come that ye may know such JOY-- and I shall be glad this day is come-- Amen and SELAH-

I am Sananda

Sarah speaking-- Beloved-- One year past I called thee together and I say unto thee ye have heard Me---

This day do ye do thyself honor-- honor have ye done unto Me.

I say ye have given unto Me cause for rejoicing--

I say I am glad- for ye have been unto thyself true- ye have gone the long way to bless them- and ye shall bless them day and night-

and ye shall be as one blest of Me and by Me- for in as much as I bless thee ye shall in turn bless them--

I say- I give unto thee that ye might be unto them My hands made manifest unto them which know Me not--

Be ye blest of Me and by Me- and I shall remember thee by day and by night

I come unto thee as thy Mother Sarah- THY ETERNAL MOTHER GOD- FROM WHICH YE HAVE GONE OUT---

COMMAND OF THEM OBEDIENCE OF THE LAW-- and they shall be brought out of bondage forever- so be it the Fathers WILL. Walk ye in the LIGHT- and ye shall be brought out--

I AM Sarah Mother of Abraham--

Recorded by Sister Thedra

Brother Bor speaking--

Blessed are thee- and blest art they who gather at this altar- continued obedience will bring greater blessings--

Obedience and order must prevail in this temple- it is upon this foundation that this temple will grow- it depends upon thee. The temple will not fail- others will take up the task if ye fail- be ye alert and walk ye in the way set down for thee and thy blessings will be in like measure--

It is not an easy task- but help is ever at thy call-- REMEMBER We- thy Sibors are with thee- and will not see thee fail if ye do thy part. In this temple all do their part- each has his place and his task.

Ye which are from this temple go in peace knowing our hand is upon thee- guiding and aiding thee--

thou will not fail if you are alert- and do not let self-will take over- for that is the door through which the dragon makes his entrance- as ye have seen--

Ye shall walk in the LIGHT I will help thee--

I am Brother Bor-

Recorded by Sorea

Beloved ones-- Ye come unto this altar in obedience and humility- the blessings shall go out from this TEMPLE to all who are open to receive--

The vibrations draw all who are of a mind to receive of the higher messages- for this is the highest- or one of the highest upon this planet- and many are not able as yet to receive of this strong meat for yet another age--

Those who are ready must be reached- none can be lost because of lack of opportunity to find their way- or heed the warning being sounded forth from all the four corners of the Earth- it must be sent forth until all hear- and either accept or deny the call to freedom--

Many are not prepared and they will have all the time they need in the place prepared for them--

But ye are the WAYSHOWERS- ye are the salt of the Earth- upon thee and OTHERS like thee- the fate of all these souls depend for their freedom-- so be ye about thy Fathers business-- and let nothing stop thee from doing that which is given unto thee to do--

Ye have been faithful- and ye shall have thy reward my obedient children- my love and my strength goes with thee- and I am ever mindful of thy needs- GO IN PEACE AND LOVE-

I Am Mother Sarah.

Recorded by Sorea Sorea

Behold me-- I come unto thee this day as one prepared to give unto thee the greater part-- have I not said that I stand ready to receive thee unto myself -- be ye as one ready to return unto me and be made whole.

I am within the place wherein I am prepared to receive thee - and many await thy coming and there shall be great rejoicing - when ye return it shall be a glad day---

Praise ye the name of Solen Aum Solen---

Praise ye--ALL THE PEOPLE OF THE EARTH-PRAISE YE THE NAME OF SOLEN AUM SOLEN- one which has given unto thee BEING---

Bless HIM which has sent thee forth for this day shall bear fruit.-

I come that ye may be prepared to bring <u>them</u> in even as I shall bring thee in-- so shall ye give unto them even as I give unto thee- for have I not said ye shall be unto them my VOICE- my hands- ye shall walk among them as myself -- as my feet ye shall walk-- ye shall administer unto them in my name- and ye shall bless them as they have not been blest---

Ye shall go out among them and they shall be healed- and they shall be lifted up- such is my word unto thee---

Now say unto them in my name- that they shall be obedient unto the law before they shall reap the benefits there of ---

I say- they shall be about the preparation of themself -- they shall be true unto themself -- they shall walk according to the commandments set down before them-- they shall go out as an example of the initiate of the temple-- they shall carry their head high-- they shall bow down unto no man-- and they shall know wherein they are staid---

They shall be as ones on whose head rests a crown- and they shall walk which way it tilts not--

Be ye not critical of them which do fall and perish- for they are but weaklings which cannot endure-- they shall wait until they have grown in spirit and in strength--yet they shall be as the little ones sleeping while it is given unto others to be up and about the Fathers business---

I say they shall not know that which goes on while they sleep-- They shall dream dreams which shall torment them--and they shall sleep a tormented sleep! Yet I say they shall awaken and come forth as the pea from the pod---

Bless the unknowing ones--be a lamp unto their feet-- Amen so be it.

I am Sarah Mother of Abraham---

Recorded by Sister Thedra

Beloved of my being- be ye blest of my being- and I say unto thee ye shall be blest this day- and ye shall bless them in turn--- I say ye shall be blessed and likewise ye shall bless them---

Go unto them in my name and give unto them this word - and they shall bear witness -- that there shall be a place wherein many shall gather for the purpose of learning of me and therein shall be a great pillar of light- wherein I shall stand- and I say they shall not be able to look upon it- for its brilliance shall blind them---

They shall fall upon their face- and they shall burry their face in their hands--and they shall be filled with fear-- for they shall have GREAT fear and trembling --they shall run and hide themselves- and they shall be as rats running into their holes---

I say they shall run as rats into their hiding places---

Be ye as ones prepared for the entrance for I shall come and I shall come - and I shall speak as man- and they shall hear my voice and they shall be glad---

I say NOT ONE shall be missed- every one shall be found and given unto - as he is prepared to receive -- I say as he is prepared so shall he receive---

I speak unto thee of this - that ye may be alert and about thy preparation- for it is now come when I walk upon the earth as the Son of God the Father sent forth of Him- and by Him - I come at HIS behest- I go out at His command - I say I go out at HIS command and I come unto thee for He has willed it---

Blest are they which receive me-- I am come that there may be light so be it and SELAH—

I am Sananda - Known as the Nazerine---

Recorded by Sister Thedra

"SERVICE"

Beloved -- I speak unto thee of SERVICE---

I say unto thee ye shall be unto them my mouth- my voice- my hand made manifest unto them--- Ye shall say unto them that in the days just ahead that one shall go out from the place wherein I am and he shall come unto thee and he shall instruct thee in the new part which shall be given unto thee-- and ye shall be unto them MY HAND and MY VOICE---

And ye shall lift them up- and ye shall heal them-- and ye shall do all manner of good works in my name-- and ye shall not want-- for I shall be unto thee all things---

I shall give unto thee that which I would have thee be---

I say I shall make of thee my emissary- and I shall give unto thee the authority and the power to lift them up- and to heal them---

I shall bless thee- and in turn ye shall bless them- so be it thy new part--- I Am Son- and A SON OF GOD- I speak for the Father which has invested within me MY SONSHIP- MY AUTHORITY- SO BE IT SELAH. SANANDA--

Recorded by Sister Thedra

Brother Bor speaking-through Sorea Sorea--

The light becomes brighter and as it shines more brightly the vibrations become higher- and those of low vibrations are greatly disturbed-- Even nature is disturbed- and you have these extremes in weather which ye are now experiencing---

These conditions will grow ever more noticeable- and more extreme--- Be ye not disturbed for as ye walk in obedience nothing shall come nigh thee to do thee harm---

Being taken painlessly from the body is not harm--ye may find it a great blessing as many have- with far grander work to do than ye could do on the earth in a physical body with many limitations.

Travel is free on the higher plane in which I fortune myself to dwell-- and we can visit many places in a short time-- with so much to be done this is a real advantage---

You would be surprised to see the things we do- and we play not- neither do we sleep—

But to accomplish our work we must have ye there doing your part-- and ye must be alert and obedient to that which is asked of thee--for ye are channels to the children in bodies who must awaken--for it is fast coming- and the time is near when they must arise and be about the Father's business lest they sleep past the time and are left behind for another age---

There will be much weeping and gnashing of teeth- but time will not turn back--and nothing can be done to ease their agony--Be ye warned---

I am thy Brother Bor

Sananda speaking---

Beloved ones-- I give unto thee this night words of living truth--WORDS that will never change---

Ye are in the last days of this PISCEAN age- and blest ye be to be part of this great time---

Many chose as did you to come into earth this time to serve- and to finish thy own tasks that ye might find eternal freedom--- Many will accomplish their purpose and return to the Father's house forever free of the wheel of rebirth---

Ye here are chosen ones- blest indeed of the Father's hand---

Ye have gone the long way - and the time of thy trials and grief is drawing to a close---

Rejoice MY Beloved Children- for ye have much to rejoice about---

Ye are doing the Father's will- ye are obedient--

Ye do that which is asked of thee with a gracious heart---

Blest shall ye be-- and as ye journey to your homes my hand will be upon thee- and I will protect thee- and all will be well with thee.

When ye have returned to thy homes ye will find yourselves in better spirit and illumination-- and I give ye assurance that much has been accomplished that ye know not of---

My PEACE and BLESSINGS I give unto thee MY FAITHFUL ONES—

I AM thy Brother and thy Sibor Sananda---

Recorded by Sorea Sorea

Sarah speaking--

Beloved Children - Children of my heart-- I say unto thee this day be ye as ones blest of me and by me-- for I come that ye may be blest-- And ye shall now say unto them which have been brought here - that they shall be as ones prepared for the greater part- and they shall give as they are prepared to receive---

Yet I say they alone are as ones responsible for their preparation

They shall obey the law--

They shall be unopiniated--

They shall be of a mind to learn--

They shall be blest for their efforts---

I say I see them as they are- and not as they appear to be-- and I I am ready to reveal unto them that which has been hidden from them

I say - I shall reveal that which has been hidden from them--- Now ye shall be unto them my hands made manifest unto them--and ye shall say unto them in my name that they shall walk in the way set for them- and they shall be unto themself true--

They shall NOT MISUSE the energy which is allotted unto them.

I say ye shall give thought unto the law- and heed that which is written---

Be ye as one which can hear me- and give unto them that which I say unto thee--

I say- THEY SHALL LISTEN FOR THE WORDS SPOKEN UNTO THEM --

They shall be as ones prepared to hear- yet they shall listen- and I shall speak- and they shall not be deceived- for I shall quicken them and give unto them comprehension---

I shall place within their hand the rod which shall become brass.

And ye shall be as my hand made manifest unto them--

And they shall be as ones wise indeed to heed that which is said- for it is just the beginning- and the preparation for the greater part.

I AM thy Mother Sarah-- Mother of Abraham---

Recorded by Sister Thedra.

Beloved -- Ye depart from this place -- yet ye shall return unto this place in the time which is near - and ye shall do thy work as ye are required in this place--- And ye will be my hands and my feet made manifest---

And ye will serve with honor - and dispatch all that is required of thee--- Unto thee will be given the gift of healing- and ye will see- and hear ---

Ye shall be able to live in this damp climate- as ye live in the desert--- Thy body shall be renewed- and in no way deter thee from that which ye are given to do---

Go ye in peace- KNOWING that I have my hand upon thee and thy Beloved Sisters-- no harm will come unto thee- if thou art faithful to thy Father Mother God- and to thy Sibors--

I am thy Brother and thy Sibor Sananda---

Mother Sarah speaking--

Beloved ones - we see thy hearts- and we know thee -- and I say ye are steadfast as the mighty ROCK- and ye are the chosen ones -- We have not chosen thee- ye have chosen to do the Fathers Will- and to serve HIM - and all LIFE- and thus ye have chosen---

Blest thou art- and blest shall ye be- and my hand shall guide thee through all things- and ye shall be unafraid---

Go thou in the Fathers service- as ye have come- protected and guided---

Be ye obedient- prompt- and ever conscious of thy Sibors- ask and ye shall receive all that ye are in need of - My Beloved Children I BLESS THEE--- I AM Mother Sarah.

Thedra speaking--- Thus closes the first year in the Service - and dedication - in the Order of Sarah. We renew our energy- and bring ourself to the altar of service as a living sacrifice - that the FATHERS WILL may be done in us- through us- by us- and for us-

-- In as much as we ask for ourself we ask for all mankind- Oh Father CAUSE it to be done--- We ask it in thy name--- Selah.

Beloved of my being -- Blest be this day- blest art thou-- I speak with thee this day that they may hear these my words-- Give them unto them which sleepeth still- and for that purpose do I come - to awaken them---

I say they shall awaken in due season--- I speak in language which they comprehend--yet language is no barrier for me-- I am not bound by any barrier-- for I am free- forever free---

I speak and ye hear me in any language- for ye have attuned thy ear unto me-- ye are my hand made manifest unto them- and ye have so prepared thyself that ye might receive me---

Now ye shall give unto them these words- and they shall hear them- they shall see them--and they shall put into their heart that which is said---

Be ye as ones alert unto that which goes on about thee and bother not with trivialities- for it is of no consequence-- for it is of no import---

That which is of everlasting and/that which is of the eternal variety shall consume thy day and night-- Ye shall concern thyself with the LAW--be obedient by day and by night- and ye shall be prepared for the place of abode wherein ye shall be free from all thy torment- all thy HELL- ye have created for thyself thy own environment- thy own torment---

None other have ye to blame-- Be ye as one which can assume the responsibility for all thyself MIS-USED energy which has been allotted thee---

I say - ye shall condition the energy which is allotted thee- for <u>every</u> <u>word</u> which goes out of thy mouth is the power and manifestation of God the Father-- it is POWER!

And ye create by the word---

I say ye prattle as fools - knowing not that ye create that which ye send out--it returns unto thee upon the ethers bringing back its kind a thousand fold---

I say ye create like unto the words which ye send out--- I say ye shall send out only LOVE and PEACE- and power shall attend them-- they shall return unto thee a thousand times multiplied- and ye shall reap the harvest there of ---

Blest shall ye be--precious JEWELS are thy words- be ye as one prepared to protect them--be ye not foolish and use them to destroy thy own PEACE!

I speak as one which knows the law---

And I say unto thee I know the danger of the spoken word- spoken in haste- and in anger-- I see the results thereof ---

I say SELF INDULGENCE is an UGLY thing! And it is a link in thy leg irons-- Self PITY is another-- <u>Self-Pity</u> is one of the greatest tormenting thorns in thy feet--be ye free from such practice! Look UP- not down---

Be ye free from all such practice--all darkness---

I beseech thee turn thy face homeward--be ye free from all thyself-created bondage - - I speak unto the ones which are of a mind to hear me- and I give unto thee these my words that ye may be free- - yet ye- <u>YE ALONE</u> can accept them unto thyself--for none other can do thy work for thee---

This is the day of preparation when ye shall be about the Father's business--and HE awaits thy preparation - and as ye are prepared so shall ye receive-- I am here--I am come that ye may have light, the bridge 'tween thee and me has been formed of LIGHT- and ye have but to cross it- it is the safe way- it is the short way---

Straight and narrow - yet SAFE- for I stand guard - and none shall be as the martyred ones- for the day of martyrdom is past---

I say that any one which cross this bridge of LIGHT is SAFE within MY HANDS! For it is given unto me of the Father to guide and to guard - protect <u>each one</u> these I call "My OWN" for they are the ones which are faithful in all things unto me-- they give me their hand-- they are glad to receive me- my word- my hand- my assistance---

I speak that they might have knowledge of me-- and blest shall they be--

So be it and SELAH--

I am the Son of God Sananda - Jesus of Nazareth---

Recorded by Sister Thedra.

TRAIL BLAZERS

Behold Me My Beloved-- I stand before thee-- and I speak unto thee in words which ye do hear- yet ye are as one blind unto my holy Christ form--

I bear my hand unto thee--I give unto thee my hand - and I give unto thee my word that ye shall see me and ye shall be blest- be ye blest of me and by me- I say ye shall be eternally blest---

I would speak with thee this day - of an example that shall be unto all men profitable-- When it is given unto man to be an example unto their brothers they are as the WAYFARER - and they are as the ones which are the TRAIL BLAZERS---

I say they which are the TRAIL BLAZERS are the ones which are the HARDY of SPIRIT--and UNAFRAID of the cruel tongues of man -- I say PITY are they which do fear the tongues of men!

I say they are the servants of the Dragon- as the ones with the VILE and pitiful tongues-- I say that the ones which are filled with fear are the tools of the Dragon-- they are UNWITTINGLY used for his purpose-- and he has caused them to fear---

They are afraid of light and truth- hence they turn away from the light-- HE-the Dragon whispers into their ear while they sleep- and says unto them- " This is not for thee- it is strange unto thee-- this is not the way of thy forefathers, they had nothing of the like--- I SAY --THEY HAD NO COMMUNICATION WITH GOD- they had no communication with the LORD - the Christ- -- What is this that they say JESUS AMONGST US? NAY NOT SO!

I say unto them-- YE SLEEPERS! YE FOOLS! YE IDOLATORS!

I say ye are befuddled--

I say ye are asleep--

Ye are among the walking dead--

Ye know me NOT!

I say ye are as ones beguiled - and ye are bound by thy creeds- thy practices of MAGIC- by thy OPINIONS- and by thy leg irons which ye forge for thyself--

I say unto thee ye are held fast by them--

I say I come that ye may have light- and FREEDOM- be ye not deceive - God is not mocked- and he which would try is the greatest of fools ---

Be ye alert and sing ye PRAISES unto Him and give unto HIM THANKS this day is come--- I speak with them which have ears to hear- I speak with them which invite me in-- I am not to be called a fraud- nor a liar- I say I am in thy midst- and I shall make myself known when ye have prepared thyself for to receive me-- and I am not deceived-- I am the SON of God - Sananda known as the Nazerine--

Recorded by Sister Thedra

"GREAT THINGS TO COME"

Beloved of My being-- I speak unto thee this day of great things to come- be ye as one prepared for this part---.

I say- wherein is it written that there shall be great changes? And great shall be thy preparation- for ye have but begun thy work--

Now ye shall record these my words unto them- and they shall receive them as ones prepared- that is- the ones which have heard that which I HAVE said- so be it that THEY shall be as ones blest of Me- and by Me--.

Now ye shall be unto Me my hand made manifest unto them this day-- and it shall be for the good of all mankind---.

I say, wherein ye are one shall come unto thee and he shall prepare thee for thy new part- and he shall be unto thee all the Father would have him be-- I say he shall touch thee and ye shall be quickened- and ye shall know-- I say thy 'front piece' shall be removed- I say ye shall remember-and ye shall KNOW---.

I am glad this day has come so be it and SELAH.

Walk ye in the LIGHT and be ye as one prepared to receive Him-- I say ye shall give unto others as ye have received - be my hands made manifest unto them--.

I speak unto <u>THEM</u> which have ears to hear and a receptive heart-- I SAY-

YE SHALL ARISE- and ALERT THYSELF- YE SHALL WALK IN THE WAY SET BEFORE THEE- YE SHALL BOW DOWN UNTO NO MAN- YE SHALL ASK OF GOD THE FATHER THY FREEDOM- and YE SHALL GIVE THANKS IN ALL THINGS--.

I say ye shall give THANKS in all things--

Ye shall walk humbly before thy fellow man--

Ye shall guard thy tongue--

Ye shall be as one responsible for all thy sorrows- all thy torment-

Ye shall be as one free from all <u>guilt</u>- <u>TURN</u> <u>from</u> <u>it</u>!

GO NO MORE BACKWARDS- turn unto the LIGHT- face it- be unto thyself true--

Speak words of PRAISE unto the Father-- give unto HIM all the PRAISE and the Glory--

Be ye not HYPOCRITICAL in thy practices- and I say GREAT SHALL BE THY PROGRESS---.

Bless them which misuse thee- give unto them nothing which they can use against thee--.

I say the Dragon uses them that he may misuse thee-- that ye may serve him- that ye may MIS-QUALIFY the ENERGY which is allotted unto thee--.

I say ye shall be alert and watchful- for there are many pitfalls- so be it and SELAH--

I am thy Sibor and thy Brother Sananda

Recorded by Sister Thedra

HOW TO "PREPARE"

Beloved of my being- be ye blest of me this day- and BLEST SHALL YE BE-- I come that ye be blest-- by my own hand shall I bless thee- such is my part-- I say unto thee as I bless thee - so shall ye bless them so be it and SELAH---

I speak unto thee that they might come to know me so be it and SELAH-

I say unto them - that one shall walk among them unknown unto them- and they shall be as ones alert that they may recognize him- for he shall be as a MAN of FLESH and BONE- he shall speak as MAN- and he shall walk as MAN- and he shall give unto them as they are prepared to receive---

It is now come when he shall walk among them- and I say unto them 'PRAY FOR COMPREHENSION - PREPARE THYSELF FOR TO RECEIVE OF HIM' - for he has within his hand the power and authority to lift thee up---

Be ye as ONES which practice the laws set before thee- and be ye as ones which speak NO SLANDER--NO MALICE--NO

ENVY--NO PART OF THY FORTUNE SHALL BE WITHHELD FROM ME -- for it is come when thy soul shall be demanded of thee-- and ye shall be unto thyself true- ye shall bring all thyself unto the altar without reservation.

Ye shall bring THYSELF as a LIVING SACRIFICE - ye shall bring thy FAMILY- thy POSSESSIONS -- ye shall bring thy EARTHLY TREASURES and surrender them up- ALL up ALL unto the FATHER MOTHER GOD-- And ye shall claim NO THING- Ye shall stand free from all earthly ties- Ye shall be as ONE FREE!

For it is now come when great things shall be demanded of thee- ye shall break thy leg irons and come free--EVEN AS I AM FREE! Forsake thy way of darkness- and ye shall be free- ye have but to follow me and I have no leg irons---

Such is my word unto thee--I say ye shall FREE THYSELF OF ALL ATTACHMENT of earthly goods-- YE SHALL HAVE NO GODS BEFORE THE FATHER MOTHER-- Be ye prepared to walk away from thy TREASURES- THY LOVED ONES AT THE CALL OF MY VOICE---

I say be ye not bound by THINGS- NOR PERSONS-- I say SERVE ye this day the FATHER MOTHER GOD - and thy freedom shall be assured thee---

Be as one which can comprehend that which I say unto thee--- I AM NOT IN NEED OF THY TRASH- THY TRINKETS OF EARTH--- I ASK NOTHING OF THEE-- Yet ye shall support my servants- that they do not hunger for bread-- ye shall support the work of <u>their hands while they are mine</u> - for I use their hands- and I give unto thee that ye may do thy part unto them---

Yet I am mindful of thee- and of thy limitation- but in my house there is NO LIMIT- no limitations- I do my part- I ask that ye do thine. I am the Wayshower known as the Nazarine-Jesus-Sananda Son of God.

Recorded by Sister Thedra

The way of the Initiate

Beloved-I am with thee- I come that ye may have my word for them-- Now I say unto them - that there are ones among them which are my hands made manifest -- I say there are ones among them which are my servants- and them which sleep NOT- neither do they flaunt their knowledge or power before the unjust ---

I say they walk humbly before thee--I say they are not puffed up- neither do they give of their wisdom unto the babbling fools---

I say they walk humbly- and gently in the 'House of the LORD'

They respect the HOUSE OF THE LORD--they move as ones knowingly-- yet they are humble of heart- and just in all their dealings-- They are BLEST of the Father- for they know wherein they are staid-

I say they from whence their blessings--they are HIS servants- and HIS EMISSARIES- so be it they are in thy midst-. I say they seek out them which are prepared to receive their inheritance - and they are as ones prepared to give unto thee the next part--I say they know thee- they see thee for that which ye are---

And they go about the Fathers business in dignity and with a glad heart-- HEAR ME! and be ye alert- and I shall quicken thee- and ye shall see and hear--and ye shall KNOW which ye see and hear---

I am thy Sibor and thy Brother – Sananda

Recorded by Sister Tedra

Berea speaking-- Beloved of my being-- be ye blest of me and by me-- I speak unto thee this day that ye may have these words for them-- and I say -- that when it is come that they are discomforted they shall turn unto us - their BENEFACTORS for comfort- yet I say it shall be too late- for "they" have set into motion that which must go into its fullness- its maturity and return unto them in its completion---

I say when they are fortuned to consume all that which they have sent out then they may be answered- and given unto as they are prepared to receive--- I say - as of other days - "THERE ARE NONE SO FOOLISH AS THE ONE WHICH THINKS HIMSELF WISE - NONE SO SAD AS THE ONES WHICH BETRAYS HIMSELF" - So be it a great truth---

Now I say ye shall give this much thought- for FEW comprehend this TRUTH today!

I say that <u>the one</u> which says NOT SO! - NAY NOT SO! and they which do criticize my word/ that of my brothers/ the word of God - KNOWING <u>NOT</u> and therefore are unfit judges- I say they are UN-learned- therefore Un-fit judges---

Blest be the ones willing to learn- willing to accept that which is said-- they which are prepared to receive the "GREATER PART"-- Blest are they which walk in the way set before them--- I say - few indeed are willing to accept the LAWS of Discipleship -- DISCIPLINE which is necessary for the preparation for the higher realms-

THERE ARE REALMS--AND YET OTHER REALMS--yet they are not all like MINE-- neither are they like THINE- there are realms dark and pitiful--- there are realms of LIGHT-- and I know the sorrow and torment in these lower realms-- therefore out of LOVE for THEE I speak unto <u>them</u> which have no light- which know NOT these things-- and I say I come that they might have light-- So be it my part with thee that they may receive from me through thy grace.

Blest art thou and blest shall ye be--

I say ye shall be blest-- I am thy Sibor and thy Brother Berea-

Recorded by Sister Thedra

Beloved--I speak unto thee this day from out the CITY of BOREALIS from whence cometh thy strength-- Thou hast recognized the power from which cometh thy help/ thy strength---

Thou hast paid homage unto thy Father Mother God--

Thou hast recognized thy BENEFACTORS--

Thou hast given of thyself that they may be blest-- and it is now come when ye shall receive of me as I have of the Father Mother God-- Blest shall ye be-- I speak unto thee this day- for the purpose of BLESSING THEM which are of a MIND to receive me - and of me-- I speak unto thee that they may be blest- so shall ye be blest that ye have given of thyself unto the light of the world---

THE LIGHT WHICH IS IN HIM which came that the world may have LIGHT-- I say the LIGHT of the WORLD is the LIGHT which is in HIM and of HIM are ye endowed thy inheritance- and of the Father which HE IS---

I say HE which came that there might be LIGHT is the Father INCARNATE-upon the earth--THE SUBSTANCE WHICH IS GOD the FATHER MOTHER - FOREVER shall be the SAME SUBSTANCE without end--

I say it is SO- so be it---

I am thy Brother and thy Sibor Michael- the one sent that TRUTH and JUSTICE - MAY PREVAIL--

I am the GUARDIAN of BOTH TRUTH AND JUSTICE - which is ONE--

And in the "ONE" shall ye work without ceasing--

Be ye blest this day---

ONES ARE IN OUR MIDST...

Beloved of my being--be ye as my hand made manifest unto them- And say unto th<u>em</u> as I would, that- There are ones within the place wherein ye are that are prepared to give unto them the water of LIFE--I say they shall be as ones prepared before they do receive- such is the law----

I say-- they shall prepare themself- and they shall apply themself-- and they shall be diligent in their application of the law -- they shall NOT wax hot and cold--they shall be steadfast in their application of the law---

I say- they shall be true unto them self - they shall be as ones which have thrown overboard their life belt when they turn aside for a moment--- Unknown unto them one shall walk in their midst and he shall be as <u>MAN</u> -- MAN of flesh and bone- he shall be as other men and he shall be as one prepared to give unto them the CRYSTAL GOBLET--

Yet only them which are prepared shall taste of its substance I say - ye have been told- yet ye have not <u>known</u> what it is - ye have not drunken of this substance-- for all which do drink shall be as one purified and made whole- so be it and SELAH

I am prepared to give unto thee as ye are prepared to receive

I am thy Sibor and thy Brother Sananda-

Recorded by Sister Thedra

Beloved - Blest art thou and blest are they who the will of the Father--- Come all ye children unto the house of the FATHER and ye shall abide there forever.

Ye have a way to go- and a work to do for the Father ere thou canst come into thy inheritance--but ye have asked to serve and now ye shall---

The need is great for workers in the vineyard of the LORD and none who desire to serve are turned away--- Oft we see that they will not be able to carry out that which they undertake to do- but they shall have the opportunity to prove themselves- and DO THEY NOT!

And so be it they shall have their REWARD- each shall be rewarded according to his works. So be it and SELAH.

Recorded by Sorea Sorea

"I am the Mother Eternal, Thy First Mother"

Beloved of my being-- This day I bless thee with my presence and I give unto thee as ye are prepared to receive---

I speak unto thee as thy MOTHER ETERNAL-thy ETERNAL MOTHER --

I speak as one which has given unto thee being--

I give unto thee that which ye can comprehend--

I bless thee in ways ye know not of--

I watch thee as a mother- for

I Am thy first MOTHER -- say unto <u>them</u> in my name--

I AM the MOTHER ETERNAL- wherein they are forever staid.

I bless them with my BEING- and I AM- and I KNOW them to be ME- and in ME- and of ME---

I am not afar off-- I am with thee- I am not cut off from thee Ye cut thyself off from me--

I say they which do cut themself off from me are as the CANCEROUS growth- which no longer conform to the harmonious WHOLE-

I AM WHOLE- yet ye cut thyself off from me by thy own wonton- thy own willfulness/ thy rebelliousness---

I say - ye turn thy face from me- and I simply wait thy return-

I am patient-

I AM LOVE--

I am WISDOM--

I am NOT fraught with UN-knowing!

I KNOW - and know that I AM--

BLEST be them which know and know that they KNOW!

I AM MOTHER SARAH- MOTHER ETERNAL AM I.

Recorded by Sister Thedra

Sarah speaking: Beloved - I bring one unto thee this day who has guarded many an initiate upon the path -- he has won his freedom and he has given of himself that others may gain theirs---

I say he has WON his freedom from the wheel of rebirth- he has gone the Royal Road within the last few months-- he was one which ascended from the HOLY MT. wherein ye are---

I say he was "ONE" which did ascend in the time since ye came into the place wherein ye are -- and I now bring him unto thee that he speak unto thee of things dear unto thy heart-- Bless this day and blest shall ye be--

I AM thy Brother -- which has come to speak unto thee of things dear unto both of us -- I am a POWATOMI Indian- and I am now guardian of many a treasure- many a secret do I guard---

I say I am the guardian of many secrets which shall be revealed unto the initiate-- and when ye shall stand before the great white altar within the holy Mt. wherein ye are ye shall be as one blest of me for I shall reveal unto thee that which ye now seek---

I say ye have proven thyself trustworthy in all things- and in all thy dealings - and ye have gone the long way to bless them and now ye shall be blest as I have been---

I say unto thee I WON MY FREEDOM--I worked long and continuously for centuries-- I walked barefoot over the hot sands from great distance that I might present myself perfect before this altar---

I say within this holy Mt. are Ones which are our Benefactors and which are prepared to deliver thee out - yet ye shall not be OPINIONATED on the method by which it shall be accomplished - for it is unlike anything known unto man - until he has the experience and then it is beyond words of man to comprehend---

I say my JOY KNOWS NO BOUNDS - I AM FREE!

Yet I stay - I am ready to stand with thee- and to bear witness of thee-- I am ready to sponsor thee in thy NEW PART- too I give unto thee assistance - and serve thee in the GREAT AND GRAND PLAN day and night for the sheer JOY of seeing the Fathers WORK accomplished---

I am with thee that it may be --

I shall speak with thee again - and again - I too bless thee---

And Praise unto our Father Mother God- Bless this day- and be ye blest eternally blest--

I am with thee -- Borachus.

Sister Thedra – Recorder

SOLEN AUM SOLEN

Beloved of my being - BEHOLD ME IN ALL THINGS PERFECT.

I come unto thee as PERFECT-WHOLE-COMPLETE---

I speak in language which thou canst comprehend—

I give that which ye prepare thyself for to receive--

I speak in ways beyond thy comprehension-for

I AM the LIFE - and

I AM the Way -- Ye are the manifestation there of - YE are ME-

Ye are of MY OWN HEART--

YE BEHOLD ME IN THEE

YE are not a part of ME—

YE are ME- and

I AM NOT PART OF NO THING--

I AM - and

I create that which I create for my own pleasure- and

I go not out- neither do

I come- I AM- and

I AM not to be denied! Neither am I of a mind to be divided- that is- in My <u>creation</u>-- THEY/IT have divided its self into many fragments- many parts- and they are as MYSELF-- yet I see them looking in far places to find me---

They deny me-- they whisper that they may deceive ME!

They came NOT for my LAW—

They wander to and fro in their sleep which they have brought about. They are as ones lost in the fog - for they have created the mist which enfolds them - it is a heavy substance which covers them.

They forego the freedom I have endowed them--

They are as ones which have gone out from me PERFECT—

They are now enmeshed in the fog of their own creation---

I have not created it-

I create PERFECT- so be it MY NATURE--

I say they turned from ME- and when they choose to return unto me without reservation- I shall accept them WITHOUT RESERVATION- and give unto them their inheritance in full-- then they shall be SONS OF GOD- which shall know as I know---

They shall have the mind which is MY MIND/the mind which shall be in them shall be the MIND which is IN ME- and I shall be glad-- so be it - they too shall be glad!

So be it I have spoken and thou hast heard me—

I AM thy FATHER GOD - so shall I ever BE thy FATHER AUM SOLEN AUM SOLEN in which ye are en-SOULED--Be ye PERFECT even as I AM Perfect---

Recorded by Sister Thedra

THE WAY SHOWER

Beloved of my Being- be ye as one blest of me and by me for I come that ye be blest--forever blest--- Be ye as one which has my hand upon thee and I shall lead thee in the way I go-- I say I shall lead thee in the way I go- so be it and Selah.

I say ye shall follow me- I go before thee that the way may be prepared before thee -- Now ye shall go as ye will-- yet - ye shall be as one blest to follow me---

I say - I shall fore-give thee the plan and ye shall be true unto thyself and ye shall be forever glad- so be it and Selah.

For them--- Now ye shall give unto them these words which I shall give unto thee for them- and say unto them as I would say ---

THERE IS ONE AMONG THEM WHICH SHALL WALK AMONG THEM AS ONE OF THEM AND HE SHALL MARK THEM- ONE BY ONE- AND NONE SHALL BE OVERLOOKED - NOR FORGOTTEN- FOR THEY SHALL BE FOUND AND BROUGHT IN--be ye as one prepared- so be it and SELAH.

I say each shall be graded - classified and put into his own category-- wherein he belongs-within his own VIBRATION-within his own environment he has now made for himself-his present-- so shall the next be like unto that which he now creates for himself---

I say he shall be WISE indeed to make it perfect- even as he would have me make for him--- I do not create for him--I create for myself that ye may <u>know</u> the LAW---

I have been unto thee the <u>Wayshower</u> - and I have said many things - in many ways - that ye be brought out of bondage -- YET - I see thee as ones waiting for a SAVIOR! I say 'SAVE THYSELF-FROM THYSELF' --I am thy older Brother which has gone before thee to point the way--I am the "POINTER". I place within thy hand the KEY unto thy FREEDOM. Ye are the one to turn it and enter in the gate-- I say it is for thee to open- and ye have the KEY --Turn it-and enter in wherein I am--and therein ye shall abide in PEACE within the LAW- so be it and Selah-- I am Sananda---

BEHOLD ME! I come unto thee this day- and I speak unto thee that <u>they</u> may have these my words--- I say- that <u>My Servants</u> bear witness of me and my hands- so do I invest within them MY WORD-MY HAND I use as I see fit-- for have I not spoken the WORD which brought THEE forth--have I not made MY WORD-FLESH-- have I not given unto THEE BEING-- Have I not proven MYSELF?

FOR I AM- and I am not to be denied-- I say unto thee, which do deny ME - "BEHOLD ME IN ALL THINGS-- I AM NOT AFAR OFF--I AM - THYSELF--I AM ALL THAT WHICH I HAVE

CREATED PERFECT-- I CREATED ALL THAT WAS CREATED PERFECT---

YET- YE HAVE dis-ORDERED ORDER--YE HAVE mis-USED MY POWER WHICH I HAVE ENDOWED THEE - YE HAVE mis-USED THE ENERGY ALLOTTED THEE-- I say- ye have gone the long way to deny me- to disprove me-- Ye have been as WAYWARD CHILDREN-- and I say unto thee ye shall now turn thy face homeward- and ye shall be received into my place of abode with great gladness--and much joy-- I AM thy Father AUM SOLEN- SOLEN AUM SOLEN-- Speak the name- there is power within it---

And I shall touch thee - BREATHE forth MY NAME- and I shall speak unto thee---

Blest art thou this day My CHILDREN- Be ye as My SONS returned unto me and be ye made perfect- even as ye went out- be ye as ones prepared for I send MY SON that ye return unto me-- REJOICE-IT IS COME!

COME - REJOICE ALL YE NATIONS OF EARTH-AND BE GLAD- AND RETURN UNTO ME-- I AM THY FATHER- WHICH HAS GIVEN UNTO THEE BEING.

Recorded by Thedra

Beloved of my Being--Be ye blest of me and by me- and say unto them as I would say - that, I am now prepared to come unto them and to give unto them as I have received- so be it and SELAH--- I say I am now prepared to give unto them as I have received- so be it and SELAH---

I say that in the days ahead that I shall go out from the place wherein I am - and I shall walk among them - and they shall be alert and they shall be as ones prepared for to receive me-- and I say- I shall speak with them - and I shall be as one of them- yet they which are prepared shall know me- and they shall be as ones glad for their knowing---

For it is now come when great work shall be accomplished in a short while- and it shall be according to the GREAT and GRAND PLAN-- I say it shall be according to the plan--and not a plan goes astray--only the sheep--so be it and SELAH---

I say- ONLY THE SHEEP go astray- so be it and SELAH--

I am with thee that ye may have comprehension so be it and SELAH.

I am thy Sibor and thy Brother Sananda.

Recorded by Thedra

THE WAY OF THE INITIATE

Beloved of My being- Blest be this day- and blest shall ye be-- I come that ye be blest- so be it and SELAH.

I say I come that ye be blest- and in turn ye shall bless <u>them</u> as ye have been blest- so be it and SELAH. I am NOW come that ye be blest- I am thy Sibor and thy Brother Borich-- and I am with thee for thy own sake- and protection- ye shall walk which way thy crown tilts not- and I shall walk side by side with thee- unseen unto the multitude--.

I say they which do not have the inner eye opened shall not see Me for I shall walk with thee in the way of the initiate- I shall make Myself seen unto them which have eyes to see- and they shall be aware of My presence- yet they shall not know Me- for I do not reveal Myself unto all men--.

I am now prepared to give unto thee a part for them and they shall be alert and heed that which is said unto them- for no idle repetition is made by the initiate- He is aware of His responsibility at all times--.

And He has within His hand the key and He alone can turn it- I say He has the power to turn it if He so wills it- So be it that ye shall give this unto them which has the will to follow in the footsteps of the Master-- Sibor Sananda--.

And ye shall add: that- He now walks in their midst as man- and He has within His hand the power to deliver them up- yet He shall find them asleep- He shall find them gaming- He shall find them within their places of entertainment- He shall find them in the places of iniquity- He shall find them at their PRIVATE ALTARS wherein they are prepared -- These shall He sup with: these shall be given unto as they are prepared--.

I say these are the ones which He shall lift up- which He shall lead out-- BE YE NOT DECEIVED- God is not mocked - He is the same yesterday and today- forever the same- I say He is not MOCKED--. I say be ye alert and be ye prepared to receive Him-- Borich

Recorded by Sister Thedra

It is true that no one can judge another's place upon the path-- much false judging is indulged in by the un-wise and uninformed children of Earth. Remember to judge not- that ye be not judged- an old rule- but ever vital and true--. .

Ye have but to look to thy own pathway that ye stumble not- and let thy brother do likewise- all have a full load to carry- do not be mindful of the loads of others- for ye cannot carry their load in this sense. Ye have help and assistance according to thy need and all will be done to help thee- be unconcerned with all else- Walk in the LIGHT as My Chelas and fear not.

I Am Sananda, Son of God.

Recorded by Sorea Sorea

Sanat Kumara speaking: Beloved of my being- blest shall ye be this day. I say ye shall be blest this day- I am with thee that ye be blest- -- I come that ye may receive the greater part- so be it and SELAH.

I say I am with thee that ye may receive the GREATER part- so shall ye receive it in this day---

Be ye as my hand made manifest unto them- and say unto them as I would say; that there are ONES which walk among them which are prepared to give unto them the water of life---

And they are now among thee as man- as woman- and they have upon them the garment of flesh--Yet - My Children- I say - BE YE NOT DECEIVED -- for I SAY THE APPEARANCE WORLD IS THE "WHORE"-- IT IS THE DECEIVER---

And it is the pitiful plight of men--- I say ye shall be alert and watchful in all thy ways--and ye shall walk seemingly in all thy ways---

For he which walks among thee will not be deceived by appearances-- and he knows thee for that which ye are--- I say; he is not deceived ---

Blest are they which are prepared to receive him---

I come that ye may all be prepared -- I say; be ye as one prepared-- it is thy preparation---And no man can keep thee out- or turn thee away when ye have prepared thyself sufficiently- so be it that ye shall see the wisdom of thy preparation - the law has been given thee - the same law which we live by- the law of LOVE and Justice; I say- LOVE and JUSTICE; I say LOVE is JUSTICE---

I say: that the LAW of LOVE COVERS ALL THY BEING--YE ARE ONE WITHIN THE LAW OF LOVE--WHICH IS THY BEING- Ye have thy being in the Father Mother God—God the first principle- the MOTHER the second principle-- the SON the third principle-- so the Father/Mother/Son the HOLY TRINITY---

So little understood upon earth---

Thou art the SON- SOUL of the PARENT from which ye get- or - have- your SON-SHIP--thy 'HAVEN of REST' is within them.

I say outside HIM the Father Mother there is no rest--there is no thing perfect-- Ye have created like unto thy own image-- ye have created thy OWN "HELL" thy own torment--- So be it ye shall now transmute all that which ye have created and return unto the PARENT ETERNAL- free.

Ye shall free thyself through the transmutation of thy own creation-- I say turn from it: as NO THING DESIRABLE! LOOK NOT BACKWARD! and be ye as one which can look UP-- NOT DOWN-- turn Not BACKWARD!

PRAISE ye the name of SOLEN AUM SOLEN forever- and forever-- give unto HIM all the GLORY forever--- I say: PRAISE YE THE FATHER MOTHER GOD WHICH HAS SENT THEE FORTH INTO MANIFESTATION---

RETURN UNTO HIM THIS DAY AND BE YE MADE WHOLE. I say: YE SHALL BLESS THIS DAY-- AND KEEP IT HOLY---

I bless thee- I give unto thee of myself that ye be blest- I am thy Sibor and older Brother - Sanat Kumara.

Recorded by Sister Thedra

Bless this day--be ye as my hand made manifest unto them: and say unto them as I would say; that there are none so small as to be forgotten or overlooked--- I say they shall be found and brought in - so be it and SELAH.

I am thy Sibor and I have sibored thee well- and ye shall now give them these words- and none shall deny them-- for I am aware of that which goes on about them-- and I am not asleep- nor am I in lethargy---

I fear not to speak frankly- for I am about my Father's business- and I have fear of no man--- Yet I say unto them which <u>think</u> themself WISE - that they know me not--neither shall they know me UNTIL they have put from them all their wonton- all their puny ways--all their cunning--all their deceit-- all their grossness--all their hypocritical ways---

I say: WHEN THEY HAVE ACCOMPLISHED THIS I SHALL COME UNTO THEM AND SIBOR THEM IN THE WAY OF THE WISE--I SHALL BLESS THEM--AND THEY SHALL RETURN UNTO THEIR OLD WAYS NO MORE!

I speak unto them which are of a mind to follow me--and I say they shall be caught up with me- so be it and SELAH. I am come that they may be---

And I am not come to sibor fools.

I say the ones which do deny me are the ones which <u>think</u> themself wise-- and there are none so foolish--- I say they are the traitors- pity are they--it is they which shall call out- LORD! LORD! HAVE YE FORSAKEN US?

I shall say - "THOU HAST BETRAYED THYSELF-DEPART FROM ME; YE KNOW ME NOT" HENCE THE PITY OF IT.

Believe in my word and ye believe in me- and ye believe in the Father which has sent me--and likewise shall ye believe in my servants---

I say: YE SHALL BELIEVE FIRST: IN MY WORK--and ye shall abide by the law which I give unto thee- blest shall ye be---

I am thy Elder Brother- the WAYSHOWER. I am the Nazarine- Jesus Christ- known herein as Sananda Son of God. So be it and SELAH.

Recorded by Sister Thedra

The ascension of the physical form is not necessary in this dispensation- this has been changed- and many will make their ascension on the inner planes through the new plan that has been worked out by those in the great SOLAR SUN who have the final say in such matters.

Ye are not to be concerned by this--Know that all is in the Fathers plan- and all will be done according to the life stream that is being carried through-- none will be overlooked- and it will be done according to the plan for each one--

Be ye alert to the plan- and do that which is given unto thee to do and ye will need have no concern for that which is coming in the future. Ascension of the physical body is for some- for others it is not- and it is of little importance which way is for thee. Do that which is at hand- and ye shall have that which is thine-- I am Son of God- Sananda.

Recorded by Sorea Sorea

"DISCIPLINE"

Bor speaking: Beloved- I speak unto thee this day as the Father of DISCIPLINE-- I say ye have done well- and ye have given of thyself: will ye not be as my hand unto them?

Now ye shall demand of them OBEDIENCE unto the law-- Ye shall be unto them that which I have been unto thee- Ye shall give unto them this discipline- and they shall abide by it---

When they come into this temple they shall be as one respectful of the priestess which abides therein--- They shall be as ones prepared for the greater part--

They shall be as ones which have come for the greater part--- They shall be as ones which come with no malice-- no hatred within them--- They shall bring with them no sore places-- caused by another-- They shall carry no hardness of heart---

I say- they shall soften their heart--- They shall be as ones come for to receive of the ILLUMINED ONES---

They shall bear witness of the ILLUMINED ONES--- They shall ask for light- and they shall receive it- so be it and Selah---

I say unto them come unto this altar and drink deeply of the water of life-- yet ye shall be as ones prepared- for it is the law--- And the Sibors- the ILLUMINED ONES THE SONS of GOD ARE NOT DECEIVED--

So be ye true unto thyself - and come as a little child- hungry for bread---

I say ye shall be as children- ask of thy FATHER <u>BREAD</u> - SO shall ye receive-- I bless thee--and I shall do myself justice-- I shall bring thee into the light-- I shall give unto thee as ye are prepared to receive- for I am thy Sibor and thy Brother- this is love in action- I am LOVE- I am thy Brother and I act according to the law of LOVE- I prepare thee for the 'GREATER PART' which is thy ETERNAL FREEDOM---

Bor has spoken---

Recorded by Sister Thedra

The climb becomes ever steeper and the way more difficult to negotiate as the time of the end comes near--- Those who are growing are finding it more difficult to walk in the way of light because of the lessons they are to learn--- Walk ye in faith knowing ye are not alone- and thy goal is near--- Fear not- and be full of JOY for thy deliverance draweth nigh---

Long the way has been - but soon all the pain and sorrow will be forgotten and JOY will be the order of the day.

Forget not thy Sibors. Look to them at all times for all that ye need. Walk ye in the light - ye children of light- thou wilt have thy reward for it is as certain as the day follows the darkest night--

In my love ye abideth- ye have chosen so, and great is thy blessing, I am with thee and I sustain thee and give unto thee all ye need.

I am thy Elder Brother Sananda.

Beloved of my being: Blest art thou- and blest shall ye be-- I come that ye be blest---

I am thy Father Mother God--- Born from out my heart art thou- - I say; from out my heart were ye Born--- I sent thee forth that ye might glorify me upon the earth---

I sent thee forth that ye might walk among them as my feet made manifest upon the earth---

I say ye shall glorify me--- And ye shall walk as I would have thee walk---

Ye shall bless them as I would have thee bless them---

Ye shall be unto them my hands made manifest- and ye shall be glad forever more--- I am with thee-- And I am not separated from thee- nor art thou separated from me---

It is now come when ye shall walk knowingly- and ye shall know whither thou goest- and from whence ye came- so be it and SELAH—

I am thy Father Solen Aum Solen.

Recorded by Sister Thedra

The peace which comes with the faithful notice taken of thy Sibors and their teachings and the care of the Sibets is a wonderful blessing- and much to be desired- for it leaves the Sibet peace of mind in which he is able to serve the plan- and to do that which he is given to do---

Ye have been given much evidence of this in the past few weeks- and ye will have more given unto thee as ye are obedient unto that which is asked of thee.

Walk ye in faith knowing the Father knows what ye have need of - and all will be given thee as the time becomes right---

All has a season- and a time- according to Divine Plan.

Ye shall be blest-for thy faithfulness shall it be added unto thee.

It is easy to find excuses--but an effort to abide by the law finds ye able to find the necessary time made available unto thee---

The willingness to do that which is asked of thee brings all other things into harmony-- and ye will find time to do all thy tasks with ease and abundance.

Walk ye in obedience to small things and ye will find the harder tasks will come more easily.

This is a testing time - if ye cannot do the small things can we thy Sibors ask of thee larger tasks?

It is thy own choice to make-- We await thy compliance in these small things.

We wait - but time is short and others may be found to do that which has been kept for thee.

Choose WHOM YE SHALL SERVE.

I am thy Older Brother Sananda.

Recorded by Sorea Sorea

MORONI RETURNS

Beloved of my being- ye come again unto this altar that ye may receive of me, and I say unto thee - I am now within my place of abode prepared to receive thee---

I say ye have prepared thyself that ye may be brought in- and I am glad- so be it and Selah.

Now ye shall say unto them - in my name - that I shall go out from the place wherein I am- and I shall pass among them and I mark them one by one- and I shall find them- for they have no hiding place---

I shall bring them in and give unto them that which I have kept for them: that is - the ONES which have prepared themself for such a part---

I say blest shall they be which do come into the place of my abode- so be it and SELAH.

I now say unto thee that ye two have been brought into this place that this work may be accomplished - it shall be!

And ye shall walk KNOWINGLY---

I say ye shall know whither ye goest- so be it and SELAH.

Ye two shall walk as ONE-

Ye shall be of ONE mind- that is-- YE SHALL HAVE NO GODS BEFORE THEE—

Ye shall BE OF A MIND TO FOLLOW ME--- YE SHALL WALK SINGLE FILE--and YES SHALL FALTER NOT-- NOR SHALL YE FAIL---

I SAY: YE SHALL NOT FAIL--- I am with thee unto the end--

I am thy Sibor and thy Brother Sananda.

Moroni speaking: I say unto thee; I come- I come- I am now in embryo- and I come as one bound by physical flesh---

I take embodiment through Morona and with the sperm of Montoya so I take physical form---

I shall speak again- and again-

I am Moroni---

Recorded by Sister Thedra

Sananda speaking: The peace of the Christ shall surround thee through all adversity. Ye shall be protected and nothing of discord shall come nigh unto thee.

Walk in faith knowing ye are protected and thou shall be blest. Obey at all times that which is given thee to do- be of a mind to be prompt to all calls given unto thee-- falter not in thy answer to all that is asked of thee.

This is the time of training- but the time is near when there will be no time to wait for those who are of a mind to keep others waiting.

Those who are directing thy action have little time for waiting. Many may be sad to find they have been left behind when the critical call is made in the last days of this dispensation- when all are too busy doing that which they are given to do, to stop and see if the LAGGARDS are coming.

In that day all will be accountable for their own part and for no other.

Train thyself to be prompt in all ye do- it is the better part of wisdom—

I am thy Elder Brother Sananda.

Recorded by Sorea Sorea

THE INITIATE

OM OM-- Borachus speaking: Blest be this day: I speak unto thee that they may know me--for I come as our beloved Master Sananda, the beloved Nazarine-- I say as HE HAS COME-- through and by the will of our Father-- that all men may be lifted up- so shall it be for the good of all mankind that I come unto thee---

Say unto them in my name that they shall be reminded of us many times - for we shall walk among them - as one of them- and they shall be alert- and they shall know us---

Yet many shall continue in their delirium- and they shall continue in their way- and not see or hear that which is said unto them. I say that they shall be as ones walking in their sleep- and everything shall appear unto them as in a fog- or a mist---

I say they shall be blinded by the mist - the veil of Maya---

I say we shall walk among them - and we shall bless them- and we shall be unto them the Ministers of many blessings- and they shall not be as ones who would ride upon our backs---

They shall be the ones who have given of themself that the Father's work may be accomplished and when they have given their all- their best- we shall give unto them a hand- in love and in wisdom- such is LOVE IN ACTION---

I say such is our part - our THANKS- our LOVE returned unto the Fathers for our Being---

I say <u>nothing</u> is <u>too great</u> <u>or</u> <u>too small</u> to ask of us, for that which we have received of HIM the Father--- and unto HIM all the Praise and the GLORY-- so be it forever---

I speak unto thee of one which has come unto thee from out the West - yet he comes from out the East and he has been greatly blest- for he shall now go his way as one knowing where he goeth-- for I shall walk by his side- and I shall prepare before him a table from which he shall choose many foods-- and each shall be palatable unto him---

I shall give unto him that which shall nourish him- that which shall be for the good of all mankind---

I say for the good of all shall I prepare for him a table with many palatable foods from which he may choose-- and I shall walk by his side - and he shall be mindful of me-- for I am sent <u>that his feet do not slip</u>—

I have said that I have been the guardian of many an initiate which has entered upon the path---

and now I have earned my freedom- I am prepared for my part- and I am glad!

So be it and Selah- I am GLAD! I shall REJOICE throughout all eternity---

PRAISE YE THE FATHER which has given unto us BEING-- SOLEN AUM SOLEN—

So be it and SELAH—

I AM - and I know myself to BE ONE with HIM-- OM.

Recorded by Sister Thedra

Blest be this day: I speak from out the heart of infinity- and from out the spacelessness of the OMNIVERSE without limit---

I speak as thy Mother--blest of me art thou---

I am thy Mother Sarah--

I am thy Father--

I am one with thy being--

I am thou--

I am thyself made manifest among them-- the difference being- YE HAVE CHOSEN TO RETURN UNTO ME- AND TO KNOW ME---

And I have accepted thee---

I have spoken and thou hast heard and answered me---

They crowd me out- put me aside-- I am not heard by them- for they have not time for me-- they give themself credit for being WISE- and I say they are as the babes yet unborn of the LIGHT---

They are cradled as the embryo within the mist- within the darkness--wherein they shall grow -- and I say they shall have their day- everything unto its season- so be it a truth---

Grieve not for them- for there is much to be done- and no time left for them for in due time they shall stir---

And one shall be sent unto them and give unto them as they are capable of receiving- so be it and SELAH.

I am come unto thee as a quickened breath- as a pulsation of thy heart- for as thy breath I inhabit thy being---

I am thy breath manifested in flesh. Be ye mindful of me- and I shall bless thee by day and by night--

My CHILD; I have kept thee for this day, and keep it HOLY- Praise ye the name of Solen Aum Solen---

I am His LOVE- I am His CREATION-

I am His COUNTER PART--His LOVE

His Hand extended-- I am the Mother Sarah---I am LOVE----

I AM

Recorded by Sister Thedra

Beloved children; children of light thou art faithful. If you remember the instructions given at Mt. Shasta, then wait until the meeting is closed to start talking; close the meeting; then ye may talk- idle talk is another link in thy leg-irons; HOW YE LOVE TO TALK! This is the time to put away thy childish ways.

Ye come here in reverence and ye are blessed for thy efforts to serve and do the will of the Father- ye shall have thy reward.

Be faithful and true; thy efforts are ever rewarded and ye shall be glad. Resentment, and SELF-PITY is unto thee, as leg-irons-- and unto thy feet as thorns, ye cannot walk in such ways and make thy goal.

I am all things to them who are faithful; look to thy Sibors for that which ye have need of.

I ever walk with the ones who ask me.

I am thy Elder Brother.   Sananda.

Recorded by Sorea Sorea

INDIVIDUALITY

Beloved of my Being: I speak with thee as thy solar sun rises over the crest of the HOLY MT. that ye may know me - that ye may be touched by my hand - my vibration ---

I say: that ye may be touched by my vibration - and by my love.

I say: we each have a vibration different from that of the other - and ye may have the gift of comprehension of these different vibrations ---

I come to speak with thee on this subject ---

As each fingerprint differs - so does our vibration - such as emanates from each of us which has been given individuality ---

I say: such is the nature of the individuality - it is different than all others - for otherwise it would not be individual in nature - for this vibration is our identity with God our Father and Mother ---

For as the atoms vibrate at the speed with all creation - we their CHILDREN vibrate like unto that which has caused us to be - which is according to HIS WILL ---

I say: that He has willed that HIS CHILDREN be perfect, like unto that which HE Created ---

Yet the child of darkness has descended into darkness and the vibration is slowed down - and the physical body is a dense gross object ---

And when man sees himself as that - as the physical man, he is but deluded by the physical eye - he knows not his source of being, the NATURE of his BEING –

I say: he has forgotten his Source - so be it and SELAH.

I am now prepared to follow through with this discourse when the time will permit thee to come unto this altar for this discourse-- so let it wait for a later hour---

I am thy Brother and thy Sibor Borochus.

THE WORD

Sori Sori -- Beloved of my being: Be ye blest this day - and blest shall ye be. Ye shall give unto them this <u>my</u> word and none shall deny them. MIGHTY shall be the WORD and GREAT shall be the BLESSING thereof. I say - GREAT shall be the BLESSINGS wherein my word is received ---

I say when one takes my word unto himself - engraves it upon his heart - makes it his OWN - and lives by it - and becomes the WORD, it shall bless him by day and by night - he shall be eternally blest, I come for that purpose - so be it and SELAH.

I am thy Brother and thy SIBOR which has worked without ceasing for many an <u>age</u> that this one may bear fruit - and it is now come when MIGHTY shall be the WORD --- the spoken word shall be made manifest before thine eyes - and ye shall produce after its kind.

So be ye aware of that which goes forth from thy lips - and be ye responsible for all thy energy which is allotted unto thee---I say it is a SACRED THING - and ye shall be AWARE of thy own responsibility and of thy own part as a creator - A CO-CREATOR with the FATHER - that has given unto thee BEING---

Ye shall glorify HIM in the earth and ye shall be unto HIM all that He would have thee be - such is HIS WILL---So be it and SELAH. So be it that it shall profit thee to heed these my words - and watch every word which proceeds out of thy mouth.

I am Sori Sori - Son of God.

Recorded by Sister Thedra

Sananda, speaking to Sorea Sorea --

Blest art thou- and blest are they who do the will of the Father- As ye obey - such will be thy reward-- Preparation time is still with thee- but soon thy true work will begin-- patience yet a little time.

Be not concerned with the time of things coming concentrate on that which is at hand.

Ye must be observant and listen for the voice of thy Sibors.

Further instructions will be given unto thee. First be observant- and do that which has been given unto ye to do- it is of little purpose to give instruction when ye have not obeyed these already given.

Blest are the obedient ones. --I am thy Sibor and older Brother Sananda –

I am Sorea Sorea. (an associate)

Be ye unto thyselves true- and all ye need shall be added unto thee. Thou art the pillars of the TEMPLE- unto thee depends the work ye have been given to do-- others could take thy place but time would be lost and time is precious unto all life at this time.

It is drawing near the time when these things must be done to bring into the outer expression that which is already expressing on the higher planes.

Ye shall work as ONE- and as ONE ye shall be blest.

The work ye are to do is not yet clear unto thee- ye are <u>not</u> to be given that which ye are <u>not</u> prepared to do---

Thy minds filled with doubts and fears could work to hamper that which w<u>e</u> are working to do---

It is better that ye be prepared before ye are given further instructions for thy work--- At this time LISTEN and be OBEDIENT to thy own promptings and to the instructions that has been given.

I am Sananda, thy Sibor and Brother.

Sananda , speaking to Sorea Sorea:

The silent night gives forth its perfume- and the day its incense of light- such is the way of life upon the planet earth-- be not unaware of the meaning behind all this- for ye are being taught to be observant.

Ye are not observant- but ye shall become observant and ye shall be assisted in this. Ye have but to listen and observe--be alert - walk not as a sleep walker- he knows not what he is doing- ye must know- and be aware at all times. Slumber not- nor dream- but be about the Father's business-- I am with thee always and ye shall not fail- be patient yet a little time. I am aware that ye have waited long --but to all things there is a season--- The time when ye shall have thy freedom is drawing close-yet a little while ye must wait- thy yearning in thy heart shall be realized and ye shall be free from thy leg irons.

Walk thee in the light my beloved child and I will ever walk beside thee and I shall lead thee home - so be it and Selah. I am Sananda.

Recorded by Sorea Sorea

Beloved of my being- say unto them as I would say - LOVE is the important thing--I say it is important that ye love one another- and all forms of life-- LOVE those who spitefully use thee- for in this is the greatest reward --ye have no special reward in loving those who love thee.

It is said that "LOVE MAKES THE WORLD GO 'ROUND" and so it is --- Be ye filled with love and no harm can nigh thy door - great shall be thy blessing.---Today thy task is to love one another- and that is <u>all</u> <u>life</u>- not just certain parts which are pleasing unto thee.

Go with my love and LOVE ALL. I am thy Sibor and Elder Brother

Sananda.

Recorded by Sorea Sorea

We who walk in the light endeavoring to guide the blind have not an easy task- for the blind are frequently very reluctant- and hard to lead---

Ye walk in the dark-would it not be the better part of wisdom to walk with faith in those who are leading thee- then when thou art satisfied that they are that which they claim to be- step out in faith - hold thy heads high and be not afraid ---

Ye shall be guided through all pit falls and dangers of every kind-- Thou shall see thy reward, the greatest thereof will be unto thee a wonder and amazement.

Be ye full of faith.

I am thy Elder Brother Sananda ---

Recorded by Sorea Sorea

To Sorea Sorea-- For the Group--

Varied are the tasks ye will be called to do--ye shall be prepared to do all that is asked of thee--I know thee - and that which ye will do.

Give unto them these words - like unto those I have given unto thee - they shall serve in many ways and they shall be prepared for their part which shall be given unto them by God the Father.

Ye shall go when called - and do that which is required of thee PROMPTLY and CHEERFULLY--No task will be given thee that ye are not prepared to do for that is the greater part of wisdom.

Yet ye must <u>desire</u> to do that which is asked of thee- for we cannot prepare thee against thy will- unwilling servants are poor servants.

Be ye of a mind to do the will of the Father.

I am Sananda - Son of God.

Recorded By SOREA SOREA

SORI SORI

Sori Sori—Beloved: I come unto thee from out infinity- boundless AM I- I am not bound by any fortune of earth- the law of earth-

I am forever free-- I am ONE with the Father Mother God-- I AM- I know myself to be---

I come as one with thee- for thou hast opened up thine heart and invited me in---

I come as the Father has willed it- that ye too may be unbound- free even as I am free- so be it and Selah.

I come that they too may be forever free-- I am and I know myself to be- there in is the difference.

They know not themself- the source of their being---

I am ONE with the SOURCE OF BEING- and I know- and I know that I AM---

Blest are they which know---

This is the first fiat given of the FATHER when He sent thee forth---

I speak as one with the Father- for all that He has is mine- I do not separate myself from HIM--

I know that which I am-- I know my inheritance- and I am glad.

I am glad this day is come when they shall come to the fullness of their estate- the ones which are so prepared---

I am thy Brother- and thou art my Sister- for ye have gone out from the heart of the Father as His breath- breathed forth into physical form- and which is but thy coat of skin- the outer garment-which is of lower vibration- which is visible unto the physical eye of the dense substance---

And I say: it is dense substance; so dense it is the deceiver-- for they see not beyond it with the physical eye---

I say open up thy heart- and ye shall see all that is hidden from thee---

Rid thyself of all opinions formed by man-- Lift up thine eyes unto the everlasting hills from whence cometh thy strength- thy intelligence-

Surely it cometh not from mans opinions: mans work- surely not thy own---

And ye shall be wise indeed to ask of God the Father for thy freedom- so be it and SELAH---

I AM- and I shall ever BE---

I am one with the Father Mother God--

I am Sori Sori--

Recorded by Sister Thedra

Borachus

Beloved of My being: I speak with thee this day for the good of all mankind- that all mankind may be lifted up--

So be it that I come unto thee as one known unto thee as Borachus- and I am with thee that thy feet slip not--.

I speak unto thee as one which has gone the royal road- and I come out of the temple of the GREAT WHITE ALTAR--.

Ye have been brought into the place wherein ye are for a purpose- and. that purpose shall be served/accomplished - and it shall be for the good of all mankind--.

I speak simply for I am a simple man-- I understand the simplicity in all things-- there are no pretentions here- it is given unto us to be simple and quiet- we are not given unto words-- for this is the favorite of the so called "WISE" and we are not part of them--- we have gone the ROYAL ROAD- whereupon we put aside all the pretense-- and we have chosen the simple way- the only way- the way that leads home--.

For there is nothing else which matters- when one sets his compass toward the North Star- I say, when he sets his compass to the point of his source- he has no other goal- he sets his attention firmly upon his destination--. he does not flounder about is shallow waters- he sets his ship on deep seas and heads for his appointed destination, knowing whence his destination--.

I say he is not divided against himself- he has not the two minds- <u>his</u> and the <u>Fathers</u>- but rather ONE mind- and he shall have no other gods before HIM- I say there is no other GOD- save the Father- and all He has is thine when ye return unto Him- then and only then do ye have the right to call thyself SON OF GOD- ye are of HIM BORN- then and of HIM do ye have thy existence- yet ye shall be

BORN of HIM- Of Light and all thy earthly substance shall be transmuted- all thy misused energy shall be transmuted and cleansed- and ye shall walk as a Son of the living God--.

Recorded by Thedra

Mission Statement

Give the truth to the world. Let it be received where it will. Many will read the messages. Some will accept the truth, others will read through curiosity, a few will ridicule. Yet to all is the truth given, and to all remains the power of choice.

The hope of the world in these times is in spiritualizing all forms of activity---promoting understanding through love and service. These must be the watchwords if the world is to come into lasting peace. We are trying to influence a world that is going astray and could cause undreamed of suffering. We are trying to overcome the thought of materialists and to bring a spiritual outlook into the earthly life. We need the help of all on earth who can think in spiritual terms. The great battle to be fought now is between the spiritual and the material, between idealism and carnalism. You can help by spreading the word---we are asking that you help because the battle may be long and the victory far away.

Halls of Light is not allied with any sect, denomination, political entity, organization, neither endorses nor opposes any cause. There are no dues for membership. Halls of Light is self-supporting through its own voluntary contributions. Halls of Light has but one purpose: to help through encouragement and understanding...

To contact the publishers or to obtain copies of our other books, please contact us at email: goldtown11@gmail.com

Sananda's Appearance

Be ye as one which hast heard Mine Voice and responded unto it - for I speak that ye hear, and I say that which is wise and prudent.

Let it be known that 1, the Lord thy God hast spoken and bear ye witness of Me, for I have made manifest Mineself that ye might know Me - and for this wast these manifestations made.

I say that I have made Mineself manifest that ye might see Me with thine mortal eyes; that ye might bear witness of Me. Yet thine companions saw and believed not; neither did they hear, for they were selfish and unprepared - yet, did I deny them?

I say; I came that they which would might see and hear. I went and came again unto Mine own. So be it that I have found; I have given unto the found that they which know not might know; that they might come to know as thou knowest.

Yet, how many hast turned from Me and persecuted thee for Mine Word. It is said, "Woe unto them which persecute Mine servants." is it not the law which they set into motion?

Yea Mine beloved, I say they bring about their own downfall. So be it that I am a compassionate one, and I would that they know what they do. So be it they shall learn well their lessons. So let it be, for this is the mercy of God, the One which hast sent Me.

So be it. I AM the Wayshower, the Lord thy God

I AM Sananda

Authority to Use the Name Sananda

Sori Sori: Mine hand I have placed upon thine head, and I have given unto thee the authority to use Mine name. For I first showed Mineself unto thee with the Word: "Go feed Mine sheep. Give unto them the name Sananda, by which they shall know Me as the Lord thy God - the Son of God sent that ye be made to know Me - the One sent from out the Inner Temple that there be Light in the world of men."

Now it is come when ones which have the will to follow Me shall come to know Me by that name which I commanded thee to give unto the world as Mine "New Name." There are many which shall call upon the name of Jesus, yet they will deny the New Name as they are want to do. While unto thee I give assurance that I am the One sent that there be Light in the world of men. Now let this be understood, that they which deny Mine New Name deny Me by any name. So be it I have appointed thee Mine spokesman; I've given unto thee the power and authority to speak for being that which I AM. And I say unto thee Mine child whom I have called forth and anointed thee with the Holy Spirit, thy name shall be as it is now called, Thedra - that name I spoke unto thee from out the eth, and thou heard Me and accepted that which I gave unto thee; and wherein have I deceived thee? Wherein have i forgotten thee, or left thee alone?

I say unto thee, Mine hand is upon thee and I shall sustain thee and ye shall come to know that which I have kept for thee. So be it that I have kept thy reward, and at no time shall it be dissipated or scattered, for it is intact. So let this Mine Word suffice them which question thee - let them question, and I shall bear witness for thee. For do I not know Mine servants from the traitor? Do I not reward Mine servants according unto their works or merits? I speak that they might know that I am mindful of mine servants, that I am not a poor puny priest who hast forgotten his servants.

I say unto them, Mine servants shall be glorified above the crowned heads of the nations which have set themselves apart, and denied Me Mine part of Mine Word - for they have turned from Me in their conceit and forgetfulness.

Now let this go on record as Mine Word, and I shall give unto them proof, which are of a mind to follow Me. So be it I have spoken and I am not finished; I shall speak again and again, and I shall raise Mine Voice against them which set foot against Mine servants, and they shall be as ones cast out. So let them ask of Me and I shall enlighten them. So be it I know whereof I speak. Be ye as ones blest to accept Me and know Me for that which I AM.

Sananda

About the Late Sister Thedra

Since the later part of the last Century the Kumara wisdom preserved by Aramu Muru has begun to reemerge into the world. This process began with the late Sister Thedra, whom Jesus Christ appeared physically to while on her deathbed and spontaneously healed her of cancer while she was in the Yucatan, where she had gone to accept her fate, and the will of our Lord Jesus Christ.

That is when something miraculous occurred. Jesus spoke to her saying, "My name is Esu Sananda Kumara" and then sent Thedra down to the Monastery of the Seven Rays to learn the Kumara wisdom. After five years, Thedra was told to return to the United States where she founded the Association of Sananda and Sanat Kumara at Mt. Shasta in California.

While heading this organization, Thedra channeled many messages from Sananda and taught the Kumara wisdom until her passing in 1992. While in the Yucatan it is said that while Sister during the 1960s Thedra was in the Yucatan, she was told a secret by her friend George Hunt Williamson, also known as Brother Philip, who authored Secrets of the Andes, and the SECRET PLACES OF THE LION.

Williamson, confided in his long-time friend Sister Thedra that he intentionally scrambled the reincarnational lineages in order to protect this next generation when they the Mayan Solar Priests, who were the direct line descendants of the Kumara according to prophesy were scheduled to reincarnate or return to fulfill their missions upon Earth, one of which was to relocate these ancient sites where the original records of the Amaru were placed for safe keeping.

Sister Thedra, 1900-1992, spent five years at the abbey undergoing intensive spiritual training and initiations. While in South America in the Yucatan, she had an experience which changed her in an instant when as it is told by her that Jesus Christ physically appeared to her and spontaneously cured her of cancer.

He introduced himself to her by his true, name, "Sananda Kumara," thereby revealing his affiliation with the Venusian founders of the Great Solar Brotherhoods. It was by his command that Sister Thedra went to Peru where in here travels she met Williamson.

Sister Thedra eventually left Peru upon telling her experience there was complete. Even before she returned to the States she met with harsh criticism from the church, which she elected to leave. She then traveled to Mt. Shasta in California and founded the Association of Sananda and Sanat Kumara. A.S.S.K.

You ask, Is There A Difference Between Jesus and Sananda? Our Lords name given at birth by his Father Joseph, and his beloved mother Mary was Yeshua, thus being of the house of David and the order of Yoseph, he would be called Yeshua ben Yoseph. The Roman Emperors placed the name of Jesus upon the sir name of Yeshua, after the Emperor Justinian adopted Christianity as the official faith of Rome, and ordered that the sacred books be compiled, upon approval of a specially appointed council, appointed by the Emperor, into a recognizable and uniform work titled The Bible. Prior to this there never was a Bible per se.

There existed until the time of the Emperor's edict, a selection of many Sacred texts, that were employed in the Sacred Teachings. Many of which were copies of what the Greeks had transposed from the original texts in the Libraries of Alexandria, which were originally compiled by Alexander the Great, and were destroyed by Julius Caesar, fearing that they might prove dangerous to the rule of a Caesar, an Earthly God.

In addition, it kept. (he thought) the knowledge of Alexander's Libraries, out of the hands of the Ptolemy's, who were said to be descended from his bloodline. At the time Caesar had no way of knowing the vast portions of the Library that were already in the Americas, in the Great Universities of the Inca, and the Maya. Yeshua spent many years in the East after his ascension. The good Sheppard, upon his appearances to the Apostles after his ascension told his Apostles that he was in fact going to tend to his Father's other sheep; which means, plainly that he was continuing upon his sacred journey. As the ascended one, Yeshua took to himself the name of Sananda, meaning the Christed one, and Sananda was thus embraced forever more by the Great Solar Brotherhood. To many of you this is all new, to others it will be received as a welcome easing of the wall that has so long separated two sides of the same coin, this is being placed into the ethers and the matrix of thought at this time as it is the time of the Awakening, and the Christos is already emerging into the new consciousness, and mother Earth herself. Sister Thedra and the phenomenon of channeling.

Authority to use the name of Sananda was given to Sister Thedra when Jesus~ Sananda appeared to her in the Yucatan, and cured her instantly of the cancer that had taken her body over. Further, he allowed a picture of his countenance to be taken at that time that she might realize the occurrence was more than a dream. Thedra had a large format camera called a 620 and it had bellows on it and founded out. She used this to take the picture of Sananda.

Sanada's Message to her by Sister Thedra. "Sori Sori: Mine hand I have placed upon thine head, and I have given unto thee the authority to use Mine name. Give unto them the name Sananda, by which they shall know Me as the Lord thy God - the Son of God, sent that ye be made to know me, the One sent from out the inner temple that there be Light in the world of men." Now it is come when ones which have the will to follow Me shall come to know Me by that name which I commanded thee to give unto the world as Mine "New name."

There are many that shall call upon the name of Jesus, yet, they will deny the new name as they are want to do. While unto thee I give assurance that I am the One sent that there be Light in the world of men. Now let this be understood, that they that deny Mine New Name deny Me by any name. So be it I have appointed thee Mine spokesman; I've given unto thee the power and authority to speak for being that which I AM. And I say unto thee Mine child whom I have called forth and anointed thee with the Holy Spirit, thy name shall be as it is now called, Thedra - that name I spoke unto thee from out the ethers, and thou heard Me and accepted that which I gave unto thee; and wherein have I deceived thee? Wherein have I forgotten thee, or left thee alone?"

"I say unto thee, Mine hand is upon thee and I shall sustain thee and you shall come to know that which I have kept for thee. So be it that I have kept thy reward, and at no time shall it be dissipated of scattered, for it is intact. So let this Mine Word suffice them which question thee - let them question, and I shall bear witness for thee. For do I not know Mine servants from the traitor? Do I not reward Mine servants according unto their works or merits? I speak that they might know that I am mindful of Mine servants, that I am not a poor puny priest who has forgotten his servants."

"I say unto them, Mine servants shall be glorified above the crowned heads of the nations which have set themselves apart, and denied Me Mine part of Mine word for they have turned from Me in their conceit and forgetfulness." "Now let this go on record as Mine Word, and I shall give unto them proof, which are of a mind to follow Me. So be it as I have spoken and I am not finished; I shall speak again and again, and I shall rise Mine Voice against them which set foot against Mine servants, and they shall be as ones cast out. So let them ask of Me and I shall enlighten them. So be it I know where of I speak. Be ye as ones blest to accept Me and know Me for that which I AM. The Final Messages on Saturday, June 13, 1992, at exactly 10.00 PM, at the age of 92, Sister Thedra made her final transition from the comfort of her own bed. When the time arrived, she simply took one small breath and slipped quietly away, without pomp or fanfare.

She left as she had lived...as a humble servant for the greater good. The messages that follow were given to Sister Thedra shortly before her transition. They are compiled here to give you some idea of the significance of her passing and of the expansion of the work, as she is now free to work unencumbered by the physical limitations and by the pain which has so encumbered her in the past. She has carried on the work here on the Earth plane for the last 50 years because that's where the work was needed...rest assured that her work now in the higher realms will simply be an extension of that work.

www.ingramcontent.com/pod-product-compliance
Lightning Source LLC
LaVergne TN
LVHW051516070426
835507LV00023B/3138